CORFU

HISTORY - MONUMENTS - MUSEUMS

Publishers: George A. Christopoulos, John C. Bastias
Translation: Timothy Cullen
Editor: Iris Douskou
Art Director: Angela Simou
Special Photography: M. Skiadaressis, Y. Skouroyannis,
S. Tsavdaroglou, S. Tselentis

CORFU

HISTORY - MONUMENTS - MUSEUMS

A.B. TATAKI

Archaeologist

EKDOTIKE ATHENON S.A.
Athens 1982

CONTENTS

CORFU — A HISTORICAL OUTLINE

The Landscape and the People

Corfu, the northernmost island in the Ionian Sea and the westernmost part of Greece, is the second biggest of the Heptanese (seven islands) or Ionian Islands after Cephallonia, with an area of 592 sq. kilometres. The island forms the largest part of the nome which bears its name. The nome also includes the Diapondia Is., the offshore islands of Othoni, Erikousa and Mathraki to the north, and Paxi and Andipaxi to the south.

Located as it is at the entrance to the Adriatic Sea, Corfu is closer to Italy than any other Greek territory and very near the shores of Epiros and Albania, being separated from the latter by a channel which is a mere two kilometres wide at its narrowest point. Its geographical position has greatly fostered its development, but at the same time it has made for a turbulent history, since the island has always been a tempting target for acquisitive aggressors.

Its relative remoteness from the centres of geological upheaval, which have caused such destructive earthquakes on Zakynthos and Cephallonia, has protected it substantially from the same fate, although it has not escaped altogether.

The island is elongated in shape, broadening out at the north end, where most of the mountains are situated. The highest peak, Mount Pantokrator (906 m.) in the north-east, can probably be identified with the ancient Istone. West of that stand Mount Vistonas, craggy and precipitous, and the slightly lower Arakli which overlooks Paleokastritsa. Another chain of hills runs more or less down the centre of the island, reaching its highest point at Aghioi Deka (579 m.). The southern part of the island, which is all flat apart from the densely-vegetated Chlomos (330 m.), includes the elongated Lake Koryssia near the west coast. Innumerable seasonal torrents collect the excess water of the autumn and winter rains; most of them dry up in the summer but the larger streams, such as the Mesongis in the south-east, run all year round.

The coastline of Corfu is very varied: much of the west coast is rocky, while the eastern and northern shores are gentler and flatter on the whole. The east coast has a number of natural harbours, two of them near the town of Corfu, and these undoubtedly played a decisive part in the initial choice of site for the town. Little islets offshore add further to the beauty of the coastline. Some of them are no more than small rocks, which are associated in folklore with the story of Odysseus and his visit to the island.

1. A Corfu bell-tower.

Without a doubt one of the main features of the landscape of Corfu is its dense vegetation, a cascade of greens of every hue setting each other off in an unending interplay of contrasting tones. Elsewhere in Greece the greenery fades or withers away altogether during the arid summer months, but on Corfu it is always fresh. Olive trees predominate — great forests of them, often growing to a great height — but the scenery is refreshingly varied with a liberal sprinkling of cypresses, a fair number of palm-trees, and shrubs of various kinds. The Eden-like luxuriance of the Corfiot landscape is mainly due to the mildness of the climate and to the fact that the relative humidity is high by Greek standards, since it rains often on Corfu. The summer heat is alleviated by the humidity (average maximum July temperature 27°C.), while the winters are unexpectedly mild, reminding one of more southerly regions (average minimum January temperature 10°C.).

It is hardly surprising that a place so well endowed by nature should have one of the highest population densities in Greece and the highest of all the Greek islands. According to the 1971 census the population of the nome of Corfu was 92,261. Corfu town has 29,374 inhabitants, while the rest of the population is spread over the prefecture's 105 communes, 98 of which are on island of Corfu. A slight decline in population during the third quarter of this century has been a fairly general phenomenon: in the case of Corfu it has been chiefly due to the drift away from the rural areas to the large urban centres. In spite of the steep growth of tourist traffic in recent years and the changes it has brought about in the economy of the island, the majority of the population is still mainly engaged in agriculture. Cultivated land accounts for almost 65% of the island's total area, and 59% of that is planted with trees. Pride of place goes to olives (3,435,492 trees in 1973). Next come citrus fruits, followed by various other kinds of fruit and nut trees of which almonds (199, 099 trees) are the most numerous. Just to see the almond-trees in blossom in January and February — massed orchards of them, set against a background of the deep blue sea and the silvery-green of the olive-leaves — is a very good reason for coming to visit Corfu at this quiet and un-crowded time of year. Grape-vines are the most important of the other crops, accounting for 7% of the land under cultivation, and some of the Corfiot wines are very good. The local market gardens produce a wide variety of vegetables; there is a certain amount of grain-farming, but only on a small scale; and livestock products play a fairly important part in the island's economy. All in all, most of the agricultural produce is of excellent quality.

The Mythical Past

Corfu was once inhabited by the mythical Phaiakes or Phaeacians. According to Homer they were a peaceful, prosperous, happy people: unwarlike, mild-mannered and cheerful. They loved to dance, play the kithara and enjoy life. The Phaeacians were the beloved of the gods. Their first king, Nausithoos, was the son of Poseidon and Periboia, daughter of Eurymedon, king of the Giants. They had originally lived in a place called Hypereia (not yet identified) but were compelled to pack their belongings and depart because they were constantly being harassed by their neighbours the Cyplopes. Scheria (the ancient name of Corfu), their new home, was an island at the end of the world where no one could molest them. There they built a fine city with high walls, an agora, two harbours and temples. Nausithoos was married in Scheria and had two sons, Rhexenor and Alkinoos. Rhexenor's daughter Arete married Alkinoos, and together they reigned over the Phaeacians. Their palace was fabulous, with bronze walls and golden portals guarded by gold and silver dogs, and the noblemen's thrones inside the palace were covered with intricately woven cloth. The royal estates, which were a little way out of the town, were full of fruit trees and vines. In this enchanted land the trees were laden with fruit all the year round, and the gods held back all the winds except Zephyr, the gentle westerly breeze, which they sent to ripen the fruit.

The Phaeacians were renowned for their skill as seafarers. Their ships were reputedly endowed with a magical power to steer the right course on their own, without captain or helmsman, and the Phaeacians frequently came to the aid of shipwrecked mariners with these vessels. This angered Poseidon, who felt that they were encroaching on his dominion and threatened one day to encircle their city with high mountains, thus cutting them off from the sea.

Odysseus was one such castaway. Shipwrecked, dripping with brine and exhausted after a two-day struggle with the waves, he dragged himself ashore on the soil of Scheria and dropped into a deep sleep on the fallen leaves among the bushes.

If Poseidon was Odysseus' enemy and the cause of his misfortunes, Athena thought of him incessantly and looked after him. While the hero was asleep, she ran to the palace of Alkinoos and spoke to his daughter Nausikaa in her dreams, assuming the guise of a friend of hers: "Nausikaa, why are you leaving the linen of your dowry unwashed? The time of your marriage is drawing near. You must wash the clothing tomorrow, so ask your father to prepare a wagon to take them". In the morning Nausikaa remembered her dream and decided to take her friend's advice. Her father, who never refused his only daughter a favour, gave her everything she asked for, and off she went with her maids to the wash-troughs by the river. The girls washed the clothes and spread them out to dry on the pebbles of the beach. Then they bathed in the river, had something to eat and began to play ball, laughing and singing.

It was almost time for the girls to leave when Odysseus' patroness, Athena, caused Nausikaa to misjudge her throw so that the ball went into the river. In their efforts to retrieve it the girls made such a commotion that they awakened Odysseus, who, on hearing their voices, decided to ask them for help. So he emerged from his hiding-place just as he was, unwashed, caked with salt, worn out by his exertions and naked but for a

The Wanderings of Odysseus

*2. In Alkinoos' palace Odysseus related the story of his ordeals
to his Phaeacian hosts. One of his most frightening encounters was
with Polyphemos the Cyclops: this vase-painting shows
the one-eyed giant being blinded while he lies in a drunken stupour.
Late 5th cent.* B. C.*London, British Museum.*

*3. Odysseus, lashed to the mast of his ship, listens to the spell-binding
song of the Sirens, mythical bird-women who lured mariners to their destruction.
Ca. 475* B. C.*London, British Museum.*

*4. Odysseus and his men escaped the vengeful wrath of the blinded Polyphemos
by roping each other to the underbellies of sturdy rams
and thus making their getaway when Cyclops let his flock out of the cave.
Late 6th cent.* B. C.*Munich, Staatliche Museen.*

2

3

4

Odysseus' Homecoming

5. *The first person Odysseus met on Corfu was Nausikaa, the daughter of Alkinoos. Their encounter is illustrated in this vase-painting, which shows the goddess Athena between Odysseus and the astonished Nausikaa. Spread out to dry on the trees are the clothes which Nausikaa and her maids had been washing. 5th cent.* B. C. *Munich, Staatliche Museen.*

6. *On Odysseus' home island of Ithaka the hero's wife Penelope and his son Telemachos were faced with some tricky problems, notably the question of what to do with Penelope's suitors. Here we see Penelope at her loom with Telemachos in front of her. Ca. 400* B. C. *Chiusi, Museo Nazionale Etrusco.*

7, 8. *Odysseus slaying the suitors with his bow and arrows. 5th cent.* B. C. *East Berlin, Staatliche Museen.*

5

6

7

8

branch which he held in front of him. At the sight of this wild-looking figure, who made a gruesome spectacle after his long fight for survival in the sea, the girls took fright and scurried off in all directions. Nausikaa alone stayed where she was, emboldened by Athena, and the long-suffering hero addressed her thus:

> *Mistress, I throw myself on your mercy. But are you some goddess or a mortal woman? If you are one of the gods who live in the sky, it is of Artemis the daughter of almighty Zeus, that your beauty, grace, and stature most remind me. But if you are one of us mortals who live on earth, then lucky indeed are your father and your gentle mother; lucky, your brothers too. How their hearts must glow with pleasure every time they see their darling join the dance! But he is the happiest of them all who with his wedding gifts can win you for his home.*
>
> *Odyssey VI 149-159*

Nausikaa answered him:

> *Sir, said the white-armed Nausikaa, your manners prove that you are no rascal and no fool; and as for these ordeals of yours, they must have been sent you by Olympian Zeus, who follows his own will in dispensing happiness to people whatever their merits. You have no choice but to endure. But since you have come to our country and our city here, you certainly shall not want for clothing or anything else that an unfortunate outcast has the right to expect from those he approaches.*
>
> *Odyssey VI 187-193*

Then she called her maids, telling them to help the stranger to bathe himself and to give him food and drink. On the way back, Nausikaa left Odysseus in the sacred grove of Athena and advised him to go directly to the palace upon entering the town, and there to fall on his knees before her mother, Queen Arete. If he succeeded in winning her sympathy she would certainly see to it that he returned home as soon as possible.

By the time Odysseus reached the palace of Alkinoos the Phaeacian noblemen were already gathered there. When they saw him appearing so unexpectedly among them and throwing himself on his knees before Arete, they all fell silent. Alkinoos even suspected that he might be one of the gods. "No", Odysseus said immediately, "I am no god. I am an unfortunate castaway longing to return to my homeland." He did not, however, reveal who he was.

The Phaeacians understood his feelings. Alkinoos gave orders for a ship to be fitted out so that the stranger might leave the following day. After lunch the next day the people of Scheria gathered in the agora and held a festival of games in his honour, with foot-races, discus-throwing and dancing competitions.

That evening at dinner-time, the bard Demodokos began singing about the exploits of the Greek heroes at Troy. Odysseus could contain himself no longer. The tears rolled down his cheeks and he revealed who he was. Deeply moved by his revelation, both Alkinoos and Arete asked him to relate his adventures to them. His account of the Laestrygonians, the Sirens, Circe and Calypso was fascinating and everyone listened enthralled, hanging from his every word. Then it was time for him to depart. The Phaeacians loaded his ship with rich gifts and other necessities, weighed anchor and sailed all night, arriving at Ithaka in the morning. They lifted the sleeping Odysseus, laid him on the sandy shore, and sailed away.

Odysseus' deepest desire and longing had been fulfilled. The day of returning to his homeland had arrived, and at last he was back at Ithaka.

Poseidon, however, was angry with the Phaeacians for going against his will. He descended upon Scheria as the ship that had carried Odysseus was nearing the harbour, struck it with the palm of his hand and turned it to stone before the eyes of all the Phaeacians who were waiting on the quay.

The "stone ship" that took Odysseus to Ithaka can still be seen off Corfu today. The imaginative people of the island have given this name to a number of rocks and islets, such as Pondikonissi (Mouse Island), near Corfu town, and a rock off Paleokastritsa. Myths and legends have remained very much alive through the centuries on the island of the Phaeacians.

The question of Homeric chronology was a matter of dispute for years, but it is now regarded as almost certain that the events referred to in the Iliad and Odyssey took place in the Mycenaean period (on the evidence of the cultural features described in them) and that the two epics themselves were composed in their final some time later, about the 8th century B.C. On the strength of Homer's description scholars have tried to place the capital of the Phaeacian kingdom in various different parts of Corfu, both on the east coast and on the west, but none of the theories so far advanced is completely convincing because no archaeological evidence has been found to support any of them: perhaps one will be given some day by archaeological research.

Another major ancient Greek epic poem, the *Argonautica* of Apollonius Rhodius, mentions Corfu and refers to the arrival of foreign settlers on the island before Odysseus' visit. When Jason and the Argonauts were fleeing with Medea from the Colchians, who had been ordered to catch them and bring Medea back to her father the King of Colchis, they too spent some time on the island of the hospitable Phaeacians. It was there, with the aid of King Alkinoos and Queen Arete — the same royal couple that entertained Odysseus — that Jason married Medea, making it impossible for her to return to Colchis. Nor could the Colchian sailors ever go back home after that: rather than face the wrath of their king, they settled permanently on Corfu.

Ancient Times

Corfu was known by many names in antiquity. The name that prevailed, however, was that of the mythical Kerkyra (Korkyra in the Doric dialect), daughter of the River Asopos, whom Poseidon had fallen in love with and brought to the island. The mythical name of the island and its people (Phaeacia, Phaeacians) is derived from their son Phaiax. Of its many other names, such as Makris, Drepane, Harpe, Kassopaea and Scheria, the best known is the last, which was the one used by Homer.

The island was inhabited during the Palaeolithic era (70,000 - 40,000 B.C.), as has been proven by archaeological finds from a cave on Mount Aghios Mattheos, in the south-west of the island. It is believed that in those days Corfu was joined to the mainland of Epiros, where its first inhabitants came from. Important Neolithic remains (late 7th milenniun B.C.) have been found at Sidari, on the north coast. Settlements dating from the Bronze Age (second millennium B.C.) have been excavated on the west coast, at Kephali, Aphionas, and Ermones; the finds from these sites give no indication of contact with the rest of the Greek world, even though, in the light of what Homer says, one would have expected some evidence of Mycenaean penetration and influence to come to light. The earliest known Greek settlement on Corfu during historical times was established about 775-750 B.C. by colonists from Eretria. Until that time the island may have been inhabited mainly by Illyrian tribesmen. In 734 B.C. a new group of colonists from Corinth, whose leader Chersikrates belonged to the royal family of the Bacchiades, settled on the same spot as the Eretrians and Kerkyra became a Corinthian colony. Built on an extremely well-chosen site a little to the south of the modern town, between two harbours known as the Hyllaic harbour (the present Chalikiopoulos Lagoon) and the harbour of Alkinoos (south part of Garitsa Bay), the city immediately found itself playing a major part in Corinth's trade policy in the west. It quickly acquired wealth and power of its own and became independent of the metropolis, although the two always remained on friendly terms. Together they founded other colonies along the coast of Illyria, including Epidamnos (the modern Dürres or Durazzo) in 625. Thanks to its trade with the cities along the Adriatic coast, Kerkyra enjoyed considerable economic prosperity in the 6th and 5th centuries B.C. and it minted its own coins. During the Persian Wars it was the second largest naval power in the Greek world after Athens, but it did not take an active part in the wars. In 435 B.C. Kerkyra came into direct conflict with Corinth over internal political disputes in Epidamnos, their joint colony. As a result Epidamnos was occupied by the Corinthians, while the Athenians intervened on the side of Kerkyra, and this was one of the immediate causes of the long and devastating war between the two rival confederacies, the Athenian and the Peloponnesian. In the early years of the Peloponnesian War, Kerkyra stood by the Athenians. Then, in 427 B.C., serious internal disputes broke out in the city when the democratic, pro-Athenian government was ousted by the oligarchs. The situation deteriorated into a civil war, which ended with the triumph of the democrats followed by a bloodthirsty massacre of their opponents. An account of those dramatic events is given by Thucydides. The democratic faction remained in power for many years. In

375 B.C. the Spartans decided to try to extend their empire in the Ionian Sea, and with the help of the oligarchs they attempted to seize power in Kerkyra, but without success. In 338 B.C. Kerkyra, which was still a major naval power, took sides with the Athenians in their resistance against Philip of Macedon.

The end of the 4th century B.C. marked the beginning of a series of misfortunes for the once powerful island of Kerkyra. It was occupied for a short time by the ambitious Spartan general Kleonymos, regained its independence and resisted a siege by Kassandros of Macedon, only to fall soon afterwards to his rival Agathokles, the tyrant of Syracuse. When Agathokles' daughter Lanassa married Pyrrhos, she took the island with her as part of her dowry. With Lanassa's help, Demetrios Poliorketes, who was as well-known for his charm as he was for his ability to conquer cities, succeeded in capturing it once more. Demetrios married Lanassa but was unable to hold onto the island, which was recaptured by Pyrrhos in 281 B.C. During this period Kerkyra, in common with the other islands and coastlands of the Ionian Sea, was frequently raided and plundered by pirates, mainly Illyrians. In 229 B.C. it was besieged yet again by a powerful Illyrian force and had to capitulate to the Illyrian Queen Teuta, who appointed Demetrios Pharios as governor. He, however, betrayed Teuta by collaborating with the oligarchs and handing the island over to the Romans. In this way the Romans acquired Kerkyra, their first Greek dependency, without lifting a finger. The island came off very badly in the civil war between Octavian and Mark Antony: the local people supported Antony, and in revenge the victorious Octavian slaughtered the children and young men and deprived the island of what independence it still enjoyed, making it a Roman province.

According to tradition, Christianity was brought to Kerkyra by Jason and Sosipater, two disciples of St Paul who were subsequently canonised. In the early centuries of the christian era Corfu is mentioned in the sources, cliefly in connection with visits by emperors, (such as that of Nero to Kassiopi), epidemics of the plague or savage persecutions of the Christians, for example, under Diocletian (284-305 A.D.).

The Byzantine Period (A.D. 337-1267)

When the Roman Empire was divided into two in A.D. 337, Kerkyra was included in the eastern section, which was later to become the Byzantine Empire. It suffered heavily from raiding expeditions by Vandals, Goths and Saracens in the 5th-7th centuries, and again in the 9th century. A raid by the Goths under Totila, in 562, was particularly destructive: it was then that the Old Fort was built and became the nucleus of the new town, the *Polis ton Koryphon* ("City of the Peaks"), as it was called in the Middle Ages.

Although repeatedly devastated, Corfu always managed to recover quickly. It evidently had ample reserves of wealth, to judge by the substantial sums of money it paid into the treasury of the state every year, and it also contributed ships and men for the various imperial wars. Administratively Corfu was a province of the *thema* (administrative region) of Cephallonia from the 8th century onwards. In 876 the Church of Corfu became a *metropolis* (archbishopric) under the direct jurisdiction of the Patriarch of Constantinople. In the 10th century the people of Corfu succeeded in repelling Slavic pirates who were preparing to ravage the island, with Metropolitan Arsenios playing a major part in the organisation of their defence. The 11th century marks the beginning of the Byzantine Emperors' desperate efforts to hold on to Corfu, whose exposed position at the extreme west of the Empire made it an obvious target for the acquisitive aspirations of the Normans, Venetians, and other European nations.

In the meantime the political situation in this part of the Mediterranean had changed. Ambitious Norman adventurers had occupied the Byzantine territories in southern Italy and Sicily, creating a nation with expansionary designs on the East. Their leader, Robert Guiscard, occupied Corfu (1081) and part of Epiros. To meet the Norman challenge, Emperor Alexios I Komnenos enlisted the aid of Venice, the other great maritime power in the eastern Mediterranean. Thanks to the intervention of the Venetian fleet, Corfu was won back for the Byzantine Empire in 1084, but those who actually profited the most from this turn of events were the Venetians, for Alexios granted them trading privileges which were to prove fatal to the Byzantine Empire. In 1147 Corfu was recaptured by the Normans, but then regained by the Byzantines with the aid of the Venetians. The Normans attacked once again in 1185, but in 1199 the island fell into the hands of the Genoese, who were the Venetians' arch-rivals, following a successful assault on it by the Genoese freebooter Vetrano Caffaro.

A few years later there occured another event which radically altered the situation in the Greek world and was to have far-eaching consequences. This was the Fourth Crusade (1202-1204), which ended in the disgraceful sack of Constantinople and the subjugation of the Byzantine Empire to the Crusaders. The conquerors then shared out the newly won Byzantine territories among themselves, Corfu being given to the Venetians in recompense for the military aid they had given the Crusaders. The island was divided into ten fiefs, which were awarded to Venetian noblemen. In return, they and their descendants were obliged to pay a yearly tax to the Venetian government, to keep the forts in good condition

9. Corfu town in the Venetian period, showing the stout fortifications of the Old Fortress and the Contrafossa (moat). 16th cent. Athens, Gennadeion Library.

10. Map of Corfu by Coronelli, dating from the period when the island was a Venetian possession. The vignettes framed by laurel wreaths round the edge of the map depict the various castles on the island, with their ground plans. Athens, Gennadeion Library.

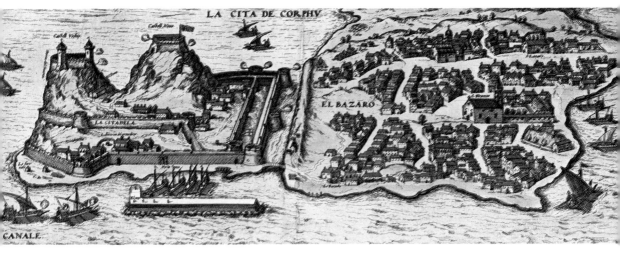

and to maintain a small military force. This first Venetian occupation of the island was short-lived (1207-1214).

In 1214 Corfu was annexed by the Despotate of Epiros, one of the three independent Greek states which replaced the Byzantine Empire after its dissolution by the Crusaders (the other two being the Empires of Nicaea and Trebizond). The rule of the Despotate marked the beginning of better days for Corfu. The privileges which had been granted earlier by the Byzantine emperors were confirmed and some new ones were instituted as well: taxation was reduced, special attention was given to the Orthodox Church, which tried to rid the island of Catholic influence, and greater emphasis was laid on fortifications and defence. It was at this time that the fortress of Angelokastro was built on the west coast of the island, to protect the inhabitants against Genoese pirates.

This phase in the history of Corfu was destined to be brief. For reasons of political expediency Michael II Dukas, Despot of Epiros, gave his daughter Helena in marriage to Manfred, King of the Two Sicilies, who was the illegitimate son of Frederick II of Germany. Helena took Corfu and parts of Epiros with her as her dowry.

Political developments in Italy, and the intervention of Pope Innocent III in the internal affairs of the Kingdom of the Two Sicilies, brought yet another change of regime to Corfu. Manfred quarrelled with the Pope, who retaliated by supporting Charles, Duke of Anjou (son of King Louis VIII of France), in his bid to conquer the Kingdom of the Two Sicilies. The two contenders to the throne met in battle at Benevento, where Manfred was killed, and Corfu was finally surrendered in 1267 to Charles I of Anjou, King of Naples and the Two Sicilies.

The Rule of the House of Anjou (1267-1386)

Charles of Anjou, who owed his throne to papal support, forcibly imposed Catholicism upon the island, and this meant persecution and humiliation for the Orthodox Church. The office of Metropolitan was abolished and his place was taken by a prelate of a lower rank, the *Great Protopapas,* who was elected by an electoral college composed of clergy and laymen. At the same time a Roman Catholic archbishop was installed in Corfu and the biggest churches were taken over by the Catholics.

The administration of the island was entrusted to a Regent who was directly responsible to the King, and the island was divided into four districts — Gyros, Oros, Messi, and Leukimmi — each ruled by a bailiff. At the same time the *decarchies* instituted by the Despots of Epiros were kept in being and 24 fiefs were awarded to barons from Provence and Italy. Thus production on Corfu was regulated according to the system then prevailing in Europe: the royal estates and church lands were cultivated by the islanders, who were serfs tied to the land. During this period Jews began settling in the town, and a Jewish quarter had been established there by the mid-14th century. At the same time a special fief was created for the gypsies who had come over from Epiros. In the last years of the Angevin occupation Corfu shared the turbulent fortunes of its rulers, until eventually, left alone and unaided, it had no option but to surrender to the Venetians, who had always had designs on the island and had repeatedly attempted to acquire it by peaceful means. The Venetians legalised their occupation in 1402, when they bought the island from the Kingdom of Naples for 30,000 gold ducats.

The Venetian Period (1386-1797)

The four centuries of Venetian rule left indelible marks on the whole way of life on Corfu. The Venetians took over an island with a powerful aristocracy and a feudal system which they upheld and strengthened. Corfu was of great importance for their supremacy over the trade routes to the Levant, and they spared no effort to hold onto it, building major fortifications to protect the island from invasion by the Turks. In return for the security they offered and for the advantages which the Corfiots enjoyed over the people of Turkish-occupied mainland Greece, the Venetians demanded complete obedience and submission. The basic characteristics of the Venetian administrative organisation were centralised government and recognition of a certain degree of autonomy, a system which was basically to the advantage of the local aristocracy. The same system was adopted on the other Ionian Islands, which the Venetians acquired later on. The highest public offices were reserved for Venetian noblemen, who were appointed by the Grand Council of Venice and held office for two years.

In the early years of the Venetian occupation all departments of the local administration were in the hands of the bailiff, but in 1420 two councillors were appointed to assist him, as well as one *Provveditore Capitan* who was the commandant of the garrison. Early in the 16th century a *Provveditore Generale del Levante* was established on Corfu with a three-year term of office: he had supreme authority over the Ionian Islands and commanded the naval force which was stationed at Corfu. Venice exercised strict control over these administrators by sending "inquisitors" to spy on them from time to time. The local government was run with the participation of Corfiot noblemen, most of whom were descended from foreigners who had settled on the island under the Angevins or had arrived later on from Italy. The nobility was subject to strict regulations which made it an exclusive caste: new members were only admitted after a meticulous examination of the candidate's qualifications, which were basically a matter of landownership and not engaging in any kind of work. In 1572 the names of all persons of aristocratic rank were inscribed in a register of the nobility known as the "Golden Book" *(Libro d'Oro).*

The highest organ of local government, the Grand Council or General Assembly, which met once a year to elect a second body known as the Town Council, was composed entirely of noblemen. The public officials

11. General view of Corfu town and the surroundings during the British Protectorate by Major Mc Niven, showing the strong Venetian fortifications, the Old

who held office for one year as judges, ambassadors to the Doge, health inspectors, etc., were all elected from among the members of the Town Council. A burgher class consisting mainly of merchants came into being fairly early on in the Ionian Islands: the burghers had certain privileges of their own and many of them eventually acquired aristocratic rank, either by amassing sufficient wealth, by marrying into the nobility or in some other way.

The Venetians always had a tendency to remain independent of the Pope, and this affected their handling of the ecclesiastical problem on Corfu. Their approach towards the Orthodox Church was characterised by understanding and tolerance, an attitude which was not shared by the Roman Catholic bishops, with the result that the representatives of the two faiths were constantly at loggerheads. Despite the efforts of the Catholic clergy, the number of their faithful dwindled steadily. The *Great Protopapas* was still elected by an electoral college of laymen and clergy, but by now he had acquired the authority and status of a bishop, though without the power to ordain priests. Tolerant though they were, the Venetians had no wish to see any increase in the influence of the clergy on the local inhabitants, because they were well aware of the role played by the Orthodox faith in preserving a sense of national identity among the Greeks.

Venice derived a considerable revenue from Corfu, not only in taxes but also from the control of the entrepot trade, the renting out of public lands, the salt monopoly and other sources. What the Venetians most needed from Corfu was its oil, so they encouraged the cultivation of the olive: in the early years of the 17th century the government was offering twelve gold pieces for every hundred trees planted, which was incentive enough to

Fortress and, in the background, the coast and the mountains of Epiros. Athens, British Embassy Collection.

make olives the main crop. This led to a decrease in the production of the other basic foods, such as cereals, with the result that three-quarters of the island's grain had to be imported. The harbour was always busy, since Corfu was a regular port of call for ships carrying merchandise from the Levant to Venetians and Corfiots with plenty of money to spend, with the result that the island's trade developed rapidly.

The burden of financial oppression at the hands of the Venetian rulers and the landed aristocracy fell heavily on the shoulders of the peasants who spent their lives tied to land that did not belong to them and had no civil rights whatsoever. No schooling was available to the peasants, whereas the townspeople had some opportunity to obtain a proper education and many young men, whose families could afford it, studied abroad at universities in Italy, mainly Padua. Armed groups of farmers, to which service was compulsory for men aged 20-65, defended the shores of the island. Some of the peasants served as sailors in the Venetian Navy, and a fair number of Corfiot noblemen were commissioned as officers.

This period was not a peaceful one for Corfu. Apart from the Genoese, who twice raided the islands unsuccessfully, the Turkish menace was becoming increasingly serious. Although Venice was losing more and more of its possessions elsewhere in Greece in its running war with the Turks, it was not only able to hold on to Corfu, but to tighten its grip on the rest of the Ionian Islands as well. The Venetians' success in repulsing the Turkish threat was largely due to the wholehearted and active support of the Corfiots themselves. The Turks made their first attempt to capture the town in 1431, when they attacked with a large force. In 1537 Chaireddin Barbarossa, an Algerian corsair in the service of the Sultan, besieged the town with an army 25,000 strong, which pillaged the rest of the island mercilessly, dealing death and devastation wherever they went; thousands of Corfiots (possibly as many as 20,000) were taken prisoner and sold as slaves in Constantinople. The Venetians coped with the serious problem of depopulation by bringing in Greeks from the territories they had lost and giving concessions to those who settle on the island. Refugees from Constantinople, Epiros and other regions which had been overrun by the Turks had started coming to settle on Corfu as early as the 15th century, but the migrations of the 16th century were more numerous and better organised. In 1540, following the Venetians' surrender of Nafplion to the Turks, refugees from that town came and settled just outside Corfu town at Kanoni, establishing a suburb which they called Anaplitochori or Stratia; these settlers were given special privileges, because the Nafpliotes were good horsemen and soldiers and Venice did not wish to be deprived of their services. At this time, too, other refugees from Nafplion built the village of Anaplades, in the Lefkimmi area, while others from various parts of the Peloponnese (Morea) established new settlements at Moraitika and elsewhere. The loss of Crete (1669) gave rise to a large-scale influx of immigrants: many Cretans settled at Garitsa, while others built the villages of Kritika, Strongyli, Mesongi, Argyrades and Aghios Markos. Thus the population of Corfu increased considerably, rising from 17,500 in 1577 to 27,056 in 1616 and 44,333 in 1706. The new settlers were assimilated quickly thus strengthening the Greek element of the population, and with their varied talents they stimulated the development of Corfiot culture.

The Turkish menace erupted once again in 1571, when strike forces were landed all along the east coast. The invaders slaughtered those of the islanders who fell into their hands and burnt down whole villages as well as forests and other property. They even entered the town itself and sacked that part of it (the *xopoli* or *borgo*) which lay outside the walls of the citadel, after suffering heavy losses. Two years later, in 1573, the Turkish army made another destructive foray into the *xopoli,* but again it was repulsed by the defenders. As a result of these two Turkish attacks, the Corfiots requested the Venetians to strengthen the defences of the citadel and to wall in the *xopoli*: this was done between 1576 and 1588. The last Turkish attempt to capture Corfu, in 1716, was one of the major events of the seventh and final Venetian-Turkish War and the last great military success in the history of Venice. The long series of wars had sapped her strength, and possession of the islands in the Ionian Sea was indispensable to the Republic's continued existence. And so, when the 30,000 Turks landed on the eastern shores of Corfu (most of them at Gouvia), the defence of the island had been planned in advance by Marshal Hans Matthias von der Schulenburg, an Austrian in the service of Venice. The town was defended by the 5000 strong garrison and by 3000 volunteers. After over a month of repeated attacks by the Turks, the defenders eventually broke the siege with a victorious sally. A terrible storm, coupled with the rumour that St Spyridon had appeared and was threatening the enemy with a flaming torch, shattered the morale of the Turks, who beat a hasty

12. The Old Fortress seen from Mandraki, with its military installations clearly visible. Athens, Eftaxias Collection.

retreat on August 11th. Ever since then a procession has been held every year on that date in memory of the Saint's intervention. This attempt on the island cost the Turks 15,000 lives.

The population of Corfu diminished considerably in the 17th century, and its economy took a downward turn. Enemy attacks were only one of the reasons for this decline: two disastrous epidemics of the plague occured in 1629 and 1673, wiping out entire villages. Two of the annual processions in honour of St Spyridon were instituted after the deliverance of the island from these outbreaks.

Serious civil disturbances rocked the island in the 17th century, taking a toll of thousands of more lives. It all started in 1610 when, after a bad harvest, the farmers refused to give the landowners their share of the produce and threatened to attack the town and free all the farmers who had been imprisoned for debt. These troubles were brought to an end through the initiative of Jeronymus Zane, the *Provveditore* and *Capetan Generale*. In 1640, however, a full-scale revolution broke out. Organised groups of peasants pillaged and looted the landowners' villas, entered the town, occupied the bailiff's palace, stormed the prison in the Old Fort and freed the prisoners. Venice then sent a large force which dispersed the rebels, but in 1642, as soon as the troops had withdrawn the rebellion flared once again only to be crushed by fresh forces sent from Venice. When further troubles broke out in the northern villages in 1652, the nobles themselves offered to pay the costs of sending yet another military force, and so a contingent of 3000 men, originally destined for the war with Turkey in the Levant, came to Corfu and stayed for three months, at enormous expense to the noblemen. The insurrection was finally put down, but only after a fierce and bloody struggle.

Corfu Ceded to the French Republic (1797-1799)

The wars with Turkey eventually wore out the Serenissima Republic. Venice was no longer the great maritime power of the Levant, and a number of other European nations — Great Britain, Russia, and France — were casting covetous eyes on the Venetian possessions, especially the Ionian Islands because of their strategic position. Within the next few years the Islands were destined to be ruled by all three of these powers, one after the other.

The ideas of the French Revolution took root quickly on Corfu, an island which had already been shaken by the insurrections of the previous century. In 1797, after Napoleon had brought about the collapse of the Venetian Republic, a French fleet was sent to take possession of Corfu. The Corfiots saw the French as their liberators and celebrated the end of Venetian rule and aristocratic supremacy. The emblems of Venice and the noble families' coats of arms were destroyed by rampaging crowds, the "Golden Book" (*Libro d'Oro*) of the aristocracy was burnt and the "tree of democracy" was planted symbolically. But the islanders were soon to be disappointed when they realised that, although they were all citizens with equal civil rights, most of the members of the Democratic Municipality, which took over the administration of the island, were drawn from the ranks of the nobility. Moreover, the economic oppression of former times was simply replaced by bloodsucking of a worse kind by the French.

The treaty of Campo Formio gave official recognition to the French occupation of the Ionian Islands, which now became a *département* of France.

Napoleon considered the Ionian Islands the keystone to the success of his policies in the Levant and had gone so far as to say that "they are of greater interest to us than all of Italy put together".

In spite of the creation of a public education department, a library and a printing press (the first in Greece), the French occupation was resented even more than the Venetian. The imposition of new taxes and compulsory levies in the form of "loans", the confiscation of property and the bad behaviour of the French soldiers, who were not paid and therefore began plundering the churches, turned the people against the French.

The Russo-Turkish Occupation and the Septinsular Republic (1799-1807)

Meanwhile the Russo-Turkish alliance had been running a successful propaganda campaign, full of pronouncements against the "atheist" French, to exploit the rising tide of discontent on the Ionian Islands. When the Russian fleet appeared off Corfu, the French were busy organising the defence of the forts and the town; anarchy prevailed in the countryside, with properties being pillaged and noblemen murdered. Since popular feeling had turned against them, the French ordered the people to be disarmed but the inhabitants of Mandouki refused to surrender their arms and so the French bombarded that part of the town and then set fire to it. General Chabot refused to surrender Corfu, but after four months of fighting the French had no choice but to ask for a truce and in due course they capitulated to the two leaders of the allied fleets, the Russian Admiral Uschakoff and the Turkish Admiral Kadir Bey. The Corfiot aristocracy was immediately restored to its former position and a temporary government was formed of noblemen and a few members of the middle class.

On April 24, 1799, the two admirals announced that the islands of the Ionian Sea were to become one nation, the Septinsular Republic, with Corfu as its capital. The government of the new state was entrusted to a Senate composed of fourteen delegates representing all the islands, which immediately took steps to draw up a constitution and re-establish the Metropolitan See of Corfu. Under the Treaty of Constantinople, which was signed on March 21, 1800 by Russia, Turkey and Great Britain, the Ionian Islands were recognised as a united, autonomous state owing tribute to the Ottoman Empire. At the same time Antonio Maria Kapodistrias, one of the two delegates representing the Ionian Senate in Constantinople, was replaced by his son John (Ioannis Kapodistrias), who was later to become the first President of Greece. The constitution of 1800, which signalled a return to the old aristocratic form of government, caused a great social upheaval which was further aggravated by the presence of foreign armies, especially the Turks. In a bid to quiet the internal unrest, the foreign armies were withdrawn from the island and the President of the Senate, Spyridon Theotokis, who in 1801 had been given special powers, invited the people to elect representatives. The representative assembly drafted a more democratic constitution, but this was rejected by the allied powers. George Mocenigo was sent to the island as the plenipotentiary of Russia, bringing with him a small contingent of troops. A moderately liberal constitution was passed by the Assembly the following year (1803), but Mocenigo managed to have it revised. The constitution which eventually came into force in 1806 recognized Russia's right to intervene in the external and internal policies of the Septinsular Republic, which thus lost its autonomy. On the outbreak of the Russo-Turkish War the Septinsular Republic took Russia's side. Eventually, under the Peace of Tilsit (1807), the islands were ceded to the French.

13. The Spianada at the time of the British Protectorate. In the centre is the Maitland rotunda, on the right the Old Fortress and on the left the colonnade of the palace built for the British Lords High Commissioners. Paintings by Joseph Schrantz. Athens, British Embassy Collection.

14. The Palace of St Michael and St George, a neoclassical building designed by G. Whitmore, is fronted by a Doric colonnade with two triumphal arches giving access to the grounds. Athens, British Embassy Collection.

15. Corfu from the south, showing the town, Garitsa Bay and the mountains of

The Second French Occupation (1807-1814)

It was on Corfu that the Ionian Islands were formally handed over by the Russian army to the representative of the French Empire, General Berthier, who dissolved the Septinsular Republic and declared the islands to be provinces *(départements)* of France. Berthier was given the title of Governor General with authority to appoint the members of the Senate. Immediately afterwards the position of Governor General was taken over by the able and scholarly General Donzelot, who had instructions from Napoleon to defend Corfu at all costs in the event of a British attack.

During the second occupation the French took an interest in the island and their presence left a good impression. Special attention was given to the improvement of agriculture and the introduction of new crops (such as potatoes and tomatoes), to the promotion of education (the Ionian Academy was founded in 1808), to the organisation and operation of public services and to planning and building construction in the town, which owes a great deal to French taste.

From 1809 onwards the other Ionian Islands fell to the British one by one. Once they had captured Paxi, Corfu was completely blockaded. The surrender of the island to the British General Campbell, and the withdrawal of the French, came as a consequence of internal developments in France following the fall of Napoleon in 1814; otherwise Corfu, which was well supplied with munitions, could have held out for much longer.

Epiros in the background. Athens, British Embassy Collection.

The British Protectorate (1814-1864)

The Ionian Islanders' longing for independence was not to be fulfilled with the departure of the French. A proposal favouring their independence was put forward at the Congress of Vienna (1815) by the two Russian delegates but was rejected by the other powers (Great Britain, Austria and Prussia). One of the Russian delegates, Ioannis Kapodistrias, who was later to become the first President of Greece, had begun his political career on his native island of Corfu at the time of the Septinsular Republic, when he had worked for the development of the economy and the improvement of education in his homeland. Subsequently his abilities had brought him to the top of the diplomatic service of his adopted country, Russia, in which capacity he continued to render valuable service to the Greek cause.

In 1815 the Treaty of Paris recognised the islands as a free and independent nation known as the United States of the Ionian Islands, direct protection of Great Britain alone. The general administration of the islands was entrusted to a Lord High Commissioner, whose headquarters were in Corfu. The first High Commissioner was Thomas Maitland (1816-1824), who at the time of his appointment was Commander-in-Chief of the British forces in the Mediterranean and Governor of Malta.

It was soon apparent that British "protection" was in practice outright suzerainty. In 1819 Kapodistrias denounced the illiberal constitution introduced by the autocratic Maitland, but to no avail. Heedless of the philhellenic spirit then prevailing in London, the British Government used open intimidation to defeat the islanders' intentions of joining in the Greek War of Independence, which started in 1821, and it adopted an equally uncompromising attitude towards the Union Movement, which came into being soon after the creation of the Greek State. It was not until after the revision of the constitution in 1848, when the freedom of the press was recognised, that the islanders were allowed greater liberty to express their support for union with Greece. Even so, the period of British rule on Corfu presents many positive aspects: economic conditions were improved and some major public works were carried out, such as the construction of a network of roads and an aqueduct bringing water to the town. At the same time education was reorganised on all levels and a new Ionian Academy, the first Greek university, was opened in 1824 under the commisionership of Sir F. Adam, thanks to the generosity of the Earl of Guilford.

The Union of Corfu with Greece (1864)

The Ionian Islands were ceded to Greece in return for the election of a British-backed candidate to the Greek throne. The Greek Chamber of Deputies duly elected the Danish prince in question, who became King George I of the Hellenes, and soon afterwards (on May 1st, 1864) the islands were united with Greece, amid great jubilation both on Corfu and in Athens.

Although the treaties accompanying the British offer stipulated that the island was to remain "perpetually neutral", they could not help being drawn into the troubled events of the twentieth century. Corfu was used as a base for the British, French, and Italian allied forces during World War I. After the defeat of Serbia (at the end of 1916), the Serbian Government and Parliament were transferred to Corfu together with some remnants of the Serbian army. The Declaration of Corfu (1917), which was signed on the island, laid the foundations of the Yugoslav State.

Corfu was struck by a bolt from the blue in 1923, when it was bombarded by the Italian fleet and temporarily occupied by Italy. The bombardment caused a heavy death toll among the civilian population, many of the casualties being refugees recently arrived from Asia Minor. The pretext for this act of aggression was the murder of General Tellini and the rest of the Italian delegates on the international commission for the demarcation of the Greek-Albanian border, who were killed on Greek soil by unidentified assassins.

Following the outbreak of war between Greece and Italy in 1940, Corfu was bombed by Italian aircraft and occupied the following year by the Italians, who at that time were planning to establish a separate Ionian State. Then the town was badly damaged in 1943, when it was taken by the Germans: several days of fighting for its possession, followed by a disastrous fire, left it in ruins. The library, the Ionian Parliament building, the theatre and many churches were destroyed at that time.

16. Empress Elisabeth of Austria: a portrait by Franz Xavier Winterhalter. This melancholy lady, a figure straight out of a romantic novel, had a special affection for Corfu, where she used to come in search of peace of mind. Vienna, Kunsthistorisches Museum.

INTELLECTUAL LIFE
ON CORFU IN THE 17TH—19TH CENTURIES

The intellectual life of Corfu and the neighbouring islands was greatly stimulated by their exposure to outside influences from many different quarters. Wave after wave of refugees streamed in from Greek territories newly conquered by the Turks, bringing with them the cultural elements of their homelands, and at the same time the Ionian Islands were wide open to Western influence, both because of their geographical position and because they were ruled by the Venetians. This combination of factors gave rise to a cultural renaissance in the 18th century, and in the 19th century Corfu was the leading centre of learning and literature, the intellectual centre of Greece.

In the 17th century Cretan artists and writers driven out of their own land came and settled in the Ionian Islands, where they imposed their own cultural standards upon the local tradition. The spread of Cretan art to the Ionian Islands had been pioneered by Michael Damaskinos, the famous icon-painter, who worked on Corfu for a number of years in the late 16th century. Later on, Theodoros Poulakis, the Tzanes brothers, Stephanos Giancarolas and Panaghiotis Doxaras all painted on Corfu. Extant works by these artists will be dealt with in the section devoted to the description of the town.

If was in the 17th century that the first Academy of the "Assured" *(Academia degli Assicurati)* was founded. One of its members was the historian Andreas Marmoras, who wrote a history of Corfu which was a major work of its time. Outstanding among 18th-century men of letters were the two Corfiots Evgenios Voulgaris and Nikiphoros Theotokis, both clergymen: they assimilated the new scientific ideas reaching them from Western Europe, but at the same time they were determined to base their wide-ranging scholarship on Greek tradition. These two "teachers of the nation" wrote in Greek at a time when the people of Corfu, or at least the townspeople, spoke and wrote Italian, since most of them had studied in Italy.

At the end of that century, the opening of a printing press in Corfu, on the initiative of the French, was followed by the publication of newspapers and periodicals in the Italian and French languages. At the same time, the educated and polyglot Corfiots founded literary clubs, or became members of educational societies. In 1808, however, the founding of the first Ionian Academy by the French had broader goals, among them being the development of agriculture and the advancement of the sciences and literature. A new library was endowed (the first one having been opened by the French 10 years before), a botanical garden and other facilities were established and a number of professorships were created for public lectures (in Italian) on a variety of subjects such as physics, physiology, politics, economics and penal law. The Academy had 28 full members and many

17. One of the main shopping streets of Corfu in the 17th century. With its high level of social, economic and cultural development, the island was a fertile breeding-ground for literary and artistic activities. The poet Solomos lived here from 1828 until his death in 1857 and was the central figure of a literary coterie which became known as the Ionian School. Athens, M. Aronis Collection.

corresponding members. All the educated élite supported the Academy — which unfortunately was short-lived — with great enthusiasm. After 1817, when Greek was recognised as the official language of the Islands (although it did not become so in practice until 1851), great efforts were made to encourage its use by promoting the publication of books in Greek, having the Bible translated into modern Greek, etc.

The cultural outlook of the island was broadened by the foundation of a School of Fine Arts (1815) by Pavlos Prosalendis, a pupil of Canova, and of the first musical societies, which soon became quite famous. The reopening of the Ionian Academy in 1824 by the philhellene Lord Guilford, who was Director of Public Education for the Ionian Islands, was an event of the utmost significance. The resuscitated Academy, which

Dionysios Solomos
The Poet of Greek Independence

*18. The years which Greece's national poet spent on Corfu coincided
with the period of his flowering to maturity. He settled
on the island after the War of Independence to lead a quiet life, and it was there
he wrote **The Free Besieged**, a major poem about the heroic defence put up
by the Greeks in Mesolonghi, which unfortunately he never completed.
Athens, National Historical Museum.*

*19. A manuscript page from **The Free Besieged**, by Solomos.*

18

was the first Greek university, functioned until the union of the Islands with Greece, when, unfortunately, the University of Athens was considered sufficient for the needs of the nation. Many famous men of letters taught in the various departments of the Academy, among them Andreas Kalvos and the philosopher Petros Vrailas Armenis, who was at the same time Speaker of the Ionian Legislative Assembly and became Foreign Minister of Greece after the Union. The historian Andreas Moustoxydis, a Professor in the first Ionian Academy, who was appointed to organise public education under his friend Ioannis Kapodistrias and was at the same time Director of the Archaeological Museum at Aegina (the first capital of Greece), was also born in Corfu. After the assassination of Kapodistrias, Moustoxydis returned to the island, where, while keeping up with his work as a historian, he held a post in the government until he was exiled by the British for his anti-government activities.

The presence of the poet Dionysios Solomos in Corfu, from 1828 until his death in 1857, marked the acme of cultural life on the island. His contribution to the literary life of the Ionian Islands was great, but greater still was his contribution to the general development of Modern Greek literature. Following his studies in Italy, he returned in 1818 to his native island, Zakynthos, where he began to do research on demotic Greek (the everyday language of the people) and used it in his literary works. When he came to live on Corfu a literary coterie grew up around him, cultivating the same living idiom, while literary circles in Athens went on trying to express themselves in their same old, dry, archaic language for a long time thereafter. Part of Solomos' long poem, "A Hymn to Freedom", set to music by Nikolaos Mantzaros (who founded the Philharmonic Society in 1840), was adopted as the Greek National Anthem in 1864.

Many members of the "school" of Solomos established high reputations for themselves in the world of Greek literature. They included Iakovos Popylas, who made his name as a critic and as a translator of the Iliad and the Odyssey, and the poet Gerasimos Markoras. Towards the end of the century the outstanding literary figure was the fiery patriot Lorenzos Mavilis born on Ithaka but educated on Corfu, who wrote sonnets and made translations from many languages. He also distinguished himself on the field of battle where he met his death in 1913. Constantine Theotokis, a contemporary and a friend of his, studied in Paris and then returned to his native village of Karousades, where he spent his life studying philosophy and writing. In his prose, which stands out as a milestone in Modern Greek literature, he observed and described the people around him, the farmers and peasants of the Corfu villages.

*20. Corfu's long tradition in painting and the fine arts was kept up throughout the 19th century. **May Day at Corfu,** by P. Pakhis, is a typical product of the Ionian school and also provides interesting evidence concerning the customs of the period.*

THE TOWN AND THE MONUMENTS

The Ancient City

Our knowledge of the ancient city is based on chance finds, excavations (still in progress) and references to Kerkyra in Thucydides' account of the dramatic events of the civil war of 427-425 B.C. (Book III). Thucydides mentions the agora, the harbours and three temples dedicated to Hera, the Dioskouroi and Dionysos.

The ancient city (which, as we have seen, was founded in the 8th century B.C.) was situated well to the south of the present town centre. The nucleus of it was in the locality which later came to be called Paleopolis, south of the modern suburb of Anemomylos. Just across the road from the gateway into Mon Repos (which used to be a summer residence of the Greek royal family) is the site of the ancient agora. The city itself covered much of the peninsula which is bounded on the north-east by the southern part of Garitsa Bay and on the west by the Chalikiopoulos Lagoon, these being the two ancient harbours: the one on the east (facing Epeiros) was the Harbour of Alkinoos, that on the west the Hyllaic Harbour. Excavations have shown that the topography of the first of these was quite different from what one would be led to believe by the present lie of the land, since it was first silted up and then completely buried by alluvial deposits. It was protected by the city walls and the narrow harbour mouth was guarded by two towers. The remains of the eastern tower have been found beneath the 18th-century Church of Aghios Athanasios in Anemomylos, for the whole of the area now occupied by that suburb used to be under water. The agora was very close to the Harbour of Alkinoos, which had shipyards and a rigging store *(skeuotheke)* along its waterfront. An indica-

21. The impressive gate of the New Fortress facing the harbour. It is crowned by the winged lion, the symbol of the Venetian Republic.

22. Reconstruction of the facade of the Temple of Artemis in ancient Kerkyra. (H. Scheif).

tion of how far north the ancient city extended is provided by the sole surviving fragment of its fortification wall: a tower still standing near the modern cemetery, which is popularly known as the Tower of Nerandzicha. It escaped the fate of the rest of the wall because it was used as a church dedicated to the Blessed Virgin. Experts believe that this tower quarded one of the city gates.

The **acropolis** of the ancient city must have been located on the chain of hills which runs along the eastern side of the peninsula from Mon Repos to Analipsis; at all events, it seems certain that there were temples, sanctuaries and parks on these hills. For the visitor traveling southwards out of town to explore the ruins of the ancient city, the first point of interest is to be found in the area of the ancient cemetery, which lay just outside the walls in what is now Garitsa. This is the **Tomb of Menekrates,** which is located in the grounds of a police station in Odos Menekratous, a street on the borders between Garitsa and the town proper. It was found in 1843, during road construction, and is a round structure of roughly-dressed stones. Its conical roof is not the original but is probably similar to the original one. The monument dates from about 600 B.C. and has an Archaic inscription reading from right to left round the top of the wall. This informs us that Menekrates was *proxenos* (consul) of Korkyra at Oianthe, his native city, which was near the modern Galaxidi; he lost his life at sea and the Korkyraeans built this monument in recognition of his services. It is interesting to observe that the ground level in the whole of this area has been considerably raised over the centuries. Evidently this was an important part of the cemetery, because two of the most interesting exhibits in the Archaeological Museum were found hereabouts: the lion which was originally thought to have stood on the Tomb of Menekrates (though this hypothesis is no longer accepted) and the capital of a column from the funerary monument to Xemvares.

The next item of interest is a fragment of the western part of the ancient **city wall,** behind the modern cemetery. This is a 4th century B.C. tower, more or less rectangular in shape and almost 6 metres high, which has been mentioned already.

A short distance from the wall, very close to the Convent of Aghii Theodori, are the scant remains of the **Temple of Artemis.** This was discovered accidentally by Donzelot's troops when they were digging a trench for defence against the British attacks of 1812. The aqueduct of the ancient city was unearthed at the same time, along with various architectural fragments and pieces of sculpture. However, the most important find yet to have come to light on Corfu, the western pediment of the temple, was only discovered in 1911 in the course of excavations by the archaeologist F. Versakis (further excavations were carried out later by Dörpfeld and Romaios). This large Doric temple (dimensions at the stylobate 47.5×22 metres) had 17 columns along each side and 8 at each end and was pseudo-dipteral in style (i.e. there was room for a second row of columns between the outer colonnade and the cella). It was constructed of porous limestone early in the 6th century B.C. (590-580), and the clay tiles of its roof were replaced with marble ones around 530 B.C. Apart from its massive altar (25 metres long), which was adorned with triglyphs and plain metopes, practically nothing is left of the temple today. To judge by the architectural fragments found in the vicinity, it would seem that the sanctuary contained various lesser buildings as well, presumably smaller temples and treasuries.

A number of important temples have been excavated in the grounds of Mon Repos (a luxuriant park, one of the most beautiful spots on the island, but closed to the public), which was originally the home of the British High Commissioners and later the summer residence of the Greek royal family. The **Temple of Kardaki,** which is the best preserved on Corfu, was discovered accidentally by the British in 1822, when they began digging to find out why the spring of Kardaki had suddenly gone dry. The cause of the trouble was that part of the buried temple had subsided and blocked the underground stream. The temple is small, Doric in style, with 11 columns along each side and 6 at each end. The east (seaward) end has collapsed into the sea and disappeared. The temple, which was almost certainly dedicated to Apollo, was built towards the end of the 6th century B.C. Some of its features present certain similarities with temples in Southern Italy and Sicily (the same is true of the Temple of Artemis, too), while its monolithic columns are reminiscent of the Temple of Apollo at Corinth.

The largest and most important temple on the island, which was most probably dedicated to Hera, also stood in what is now the Mon Repos estate. Nothing of it is left in situ, but a number of architectural fragments have been found, and from these it can be dated to the late 7th century B.C. It seems that the temple was destroyed towards the end of the 5th century B.C., most probably during the civil wars, and then rebuilt about 400 B.C. The Temple of Hera is referred to by Thucydides in his account of the extermination of the oligarchs by their opponents. Two smaller temples also stood in this sanctuary. Finds from these buildings and from others excavated in different parts of the ancient city — including several houses, one small shrine and the Roman baths — may be seen in the Archaeological Museum.

Early Christian and Byzantine Monuments near the Town

The **basilica of Paleopolis,** also known as Aghia Kerkyra, is located close to the entrance of Mon Repos, in what was the centre of the ancient city. Material from earlier buildings was used in the construction of the first large five-naved basilica (5th century A.D.), of which only the outer walls are still standing. This church was destroyed during the invasions of the 6th century and soon replaced by a smaller basilica, which was itself destroyed in the invasions of the 11th century and then rebuilt, on a still smaller scale the following century. It was renovated once again in 1537 but finally destroyed by bombing in the Second World War, and so we know its final form only from drawings of the 17th century. The buildings which occupied this site before the first basilica, and from which materials were "borrowed" for the successive churches, were a Doric temple of the 5th century B.C. and a Roman odeum among others. An inscription in hexameters on the architrave over the west door of the basilica informs us that Jovian, Bishop of Corfu, built this church in the 5th century after demolishing the pagan altars on the site. Pieces of the mosaic floor and architectural fragments from the basilica may be seen in the Collection of Christian Art in the Palace.

After the barbarian raids of the 6th century the inhabitants gradually drifted away from the ancient city, and took refuge on the promontory where the Old Fort now stands, which eventually became the new town centre. This new town was already walled by the 10th century, and the Old Tower - the *Torre del Mar* of the Venetians - was built at that time on one of its two peaks. It was then, too, that a suburb started growing up outside the walls, on the site to which the town was moved later on. The Byzantine

23. The Tomb of Menekrates is a circular building with a conical roof, dating from ca. 600 B.C.

period on Corfu is represented by a number of fortifications in the countryside (which will be dealt with elsewhere) and by a solitary Byzantine church, which was also outside the town at the time when it was built but will be described here for the sake of historical continuity. This church, which was once the *katholikon* of a monastery, is located at Garitsa and is dedicated to **SS Jason and Sosipater,** who are traditionally held to have brought Christianity to the island. It is a cruciform church with an octagonal dome. Inside the church there are two monolithic columns of green stone, while the outside walls are decorated with courses of tiles. It was dated to the 12th century, but modern opinion assigns it to an earlier date, about the year 1000. In the narthex is the one and only surviving fresco, recently dated to the 11th century, which depicts St Arsenios, the tenth-century Bishop of Corfu. The icons of the church's two patron saints are attributed to the great Cretan painter, Michael Damaskinos, who worked on Corfu in the late 16th century.

Another Cretan painter, Emmanuel Tzane Bounialis, also worked on the island in the mid-17th century and painted many icons in this church. One of them, depicting St Cyril, Patriarch of Alexandria, has been taken to the Museum in the Palace, while the icons of St John Damascene and St Gregory may still be seen in the church. Also kept there is an embroidered

24. The Church of SS Jason and Sosipater is the most typical monument of the Byzantine period. The icons of the church's two patron saints are attributed to the Cretan painter Michael Damaskinos (late 16th cent.).

robe that belonged to Catherine Paleologos (wife of Thomas, the last Despot of the Morea), who fled for refuge to the monastery and ended her days there.

The Town During the Venetian Period

The town owes more of its characteristic features to the four centuries of Venetian rule than to any other period before or since. It is to Venice that Corfu owes its unique character, which consists in the preservation, in appearance at least, of a past which has left a profound mark on Corfiot life. As you walk along the *kandounia* (streets and alleyways) of Corfu town or wander around the forts, it is easy to be carried back a few centuries without having the feeling of being in a museum: the basic town plan is the same as it was a few hundred years ago; the houses are still inhabited, even if their appearance may have changed to a greater or lesser extend; the churches still stand where they were, usually with a piazza in front of them; and the forts still contain military installations which make it impossible for the casual visitor to explore their secrets, just as they did in Venetian times. Any gaps in these pictures are due to the bombing raids of the last war and the new buildings constructed in recent years, which all too often, alas, show a total disregard for the unique character of the town.

Fortifications

The Venetian fortifications, built to defend Corfu against the ever-present danger of attack from one quarter or another, still dominate the town. The earliest of them was constructed in the 15th century, the latest in the final century of Venetian rule. Confined as it was within its bastioned walls, the town could not grow outwards but only upwards, which accounts for the number of multi-storey buildings packed together along the narrow streets. At first only the citadel was fortified, while the settlement which had grown up outside, the *xopoli* or *borgo,* was left unwalled. One of the first works to be carried out was the digging of the *Contrafossa,* the moat which transformed the peninsula of the citadel into a man-made island. Early in the 15th century, as we know from contemporary plans and maps, two walls were built to replace the Byzantine fortifications, one near the water's edge and the other higher up around the two peaks *(korfi)* which by this time had given their name to the new town. With the evolution of new military tactics, however, and after the heavy losses sustained in the siege of 1537, the fortifications were modernised and extended so as to protect the houses outside the citadel. The major alterations were carried out in the years between the two Turkish sieges (1537 & 1571): it was then that the two bastions of the Old Fort and the wall between them were constructed, overlooking the moat, which was widened at the same time. The only access from the mainland was by means of a drawbridge. The two bastions were named after the garrison commandants, Martinengo and Savorgnan. The open space between the citadel and the *xopoli* was enlarged to give the defenders a clear field of fire: this open ground, where no building was allowed, became the *Esplanade* (Spianada). The architect Michele Sanmicheli, an authority on the building of new-style bastions capable of withstanding artillery bombardment, was in charge of this reconstruction programme to start with; he was later replaced by his nephew Giangirolamo Sanmicheli. The second Turkish siege (1571) noted the beginning of a new phase in the town's defence-works, mainly concerned with the construction of a wall to protect the west side of the *xopoli*. To make it possible for the necessary walls and fortifications to be built, the people of the outlying suburb of Sarokko were forced to demolish approximately 2000 buildings. The western end of the wall terminated at the **New Fort,** (Fortezza Nuova) which was completed in 1576, although the whole circuit was not completed until 1588. There were four gates leading out of the town: two on the seaward side - the Spilia Gate (Gate of the Cave) at the eastern end of the New Fort and the St Nicholas Gate at the north end of the Spianada - and two on the landward side - the Royal Gate *(Porta Reale)* leading out to Sarokko and the rest of the island, and the Raimonda Gate leading to Garitsa. The first two are still standing: the St Nicholas Gate at the foot of the wall, now out of sight below the level of the seafront road, is the more impressive. The Porta Reale, which was the most attractive of the four, and the Raimonda Gate were both demolished in the 19th century to accommodate the traffic. This phase of the construction programme was supervised by the engineer Ferrante Vitelli. The basic fortifications were supplemented in the 17th century by the construction of a second line of defence, and again in the 18th century when the Avrami and Sotiros hills were fortified after the siege of 1716 under the supervision of Count Schulenburg.

Once the town had been walled only a few houses were left in the Old Fort, and in time these and the churches in the citadel were all abandoned, although the offices of the town administration remained there. The Venetian walls of the Old Fort are still standing today, as well as the additional fortifications erected by the British. Since it is still used by the army, entrance is permitted only at certain hours of the day and visitors may only go as far as the Church of St George. The walls of the fort are on three levels, the first surrounding the two peaks and the second enclosing most of the promontory, while the third is a sea castle on Cape Kavosidero, at the northeast point of the promontory. A fixed iron bridge 60 metres long has replaced the old drawbridge.

Entering the citadel through the fine vaulted gateway, you emerge into a piazza, at the far end of which stood the residence of the *Provveditore,* though this has been demolished along with most of the other Venetian buildings in the fort. The palace of the *Provveditore Generale* stood on the north side of the piazza, overlooking the harbour of Mandraki. Its ground floor was used as a prison. The other buildings were warehouses, barrack-blocks and an arsenal. The two towers, known as the Land Tower and the Sea Tower, are still standing in good condition in the centre of the promontory, with a Venetian prison building near the first and British barrack-blocks between the two. In 1840 the British built the **Church of St George** on the lower ground in the southern part of the fort. It is modelled on a Doric temple, and the first time one's eyes stray in this direction it comes as something of a shock to see the mixture of architectural styles in this part of the citadel.

Description of the Town: Public and Private Buildings

The walled town was confined within an area of 295 hectares (about 73 acres), although it could have expanded naturally in three directions: to the suburbs of Garitsa southwards along the sea, Sarokko between the hills of Avrami and Sotiros, and Mandouki to the northwest. The Spianada takes up one-third of the total area of the town, and in the Venetian period it was not used as a public promenade but as a means of defence. The town has many squares, or rather irregularly-shaped church piazzas, all much smaller than the Spianada of course, which provided essential breathing-spaces among the closely-packed houses. In its planning, as well as the appearance of its buildings, Corfu resembles Venice. It was only natural that Corfu should fall under the artistic influence of the metropolis, and equally natural that its expansion should follow the contours of the land, the hills and valleys which gave the town its shape.

On the three main hills, Campiello in the northeast of the town, is the most densely built-up and is also distinguished for the fine architecture of some of its buildings. It was regarded as the best neighbourhood and many of the noblemen had their homes there. The three sections of the town were divided into a large number of small neighbourhoods, each centred round a church from which it usually took its name. The two main streets, Odos Evgeniou Voulgareos and Odos Nikiphorou Theotoki, are in the lower part of the town, which is the commercial centre. The shopping streets — those two plus Odos Michail Theotoki and Odos Filarmonikis — are remarkable for their *volta* (arcaded pavements), which give the pedestrians room to walk in safety and in shelter, clear of the busy traffic and protected against the weather, without reducing the floor space of the upper storeys on both sides of the street. The colonnades, which are supported on stone piers, are one of the most picturesque features on the town. Odos Moustoxydi, which is still referred to locally as *Platy Kandouni* after its Italian name of *Strada Larga* (Broad Street), used to be one of the main thoroughfares. It was much wider in the past, and at Carnival time it used to be used for contests of horsemanship which were survivals from the bloodthirsty tournaments and duels of the Middle Ages. These jousting displays *(Giostre* or *Chiostra Pubblica)* were great occasions for the townspeople and were of two kinds: in one the contestants had to run their lances through a ring suspended at the roadside, while in the other they had to charge at a dummy and run it through. The contests were judged by the *Provveditore* and the *Sindichi,* who stood on the balcony of the Ricchi mansion. The winner received a prize and was given a hero's ovation by the spectators, who were packed tight on the pavement all along the street or, if they were lucky, on balconies or leaning out of the upper windows. Only noblemen participated in the jousting, and they were forbidden to wear masks or fancy dress as was customary during the Carnival.

The most important piazza in the town was the gently sloping square in front of the building which is now the Town Hall and used to be the **Lodge of the Nobles** *(Loggia Nobilei).* The 17th-century Catholic Cathedral of St James and the palace of the Catholic Archbishop both open on to this square, which was the social centre of the town. Another important building, now destroyed, was the residence of the bailiff, which occupied the site where the Second Primary School now stands. Thus, in this square, one may see two of the four surviving Venetian public buildings. The Lodge of the Nobles, constructed of Sinies stone, is the only building with chiselled masonry and the most elaborately ornamented edifice in the town. It took thirty years to build, starting in 1663. In 1691 the bust of Morosini, surrounded by four children symbolizing his virtues, was immured in its east wall. In 1720 the Lodge was converted into a theatre, which was named San Giacomo and was used initially for the entertainment of naval officers and later (from 1773) as an opera house. In the early years of this century a new theatre was built (it was destroyed in 1943), while the Lodge, with one extra floor added, became the Town Hall. The **Catholic Archbishop's Palace** was originally built in the 17th century but rebuilt in the 18th and has had many alterations made to it since then. It was used for some time as the Law Courts and has recently become the local branch of the Bank of Greece. The other two Venetian public buildings still standing were originally barrack-blocks. One is at the southern end of the Spianada, near the site of the demolished Raimonda Gate, and was known as the **Pasqualigo** or **Grimani Barracks.** In 1840 the Ionian Academy was transferred here, while later on it housed the Municipal Library. This large, three-storey building was destroyed by bombing in 1943, but even in its ruined state it is still imposing, its main features being simplicity and symmetry. The **Spilia Barracks** near the New Fort, the fourth and last of these public buildings, is now the Agricultural Bank of Greece. Another notable building of the Venetian period which, like the bailiff's palace, is no longer standing, was the Lodge where the Grand Council of Corfu town held its meetings. This stood on the Spianada, near the Old Fort. The Pawn Exchange was located to the north of it with the military hospital close by, a little way up from the St Nicholas Gate.

Apart from the public buildings, the town derives its distinctive character from the many residential blocks still standing, most of them dating from the 17th and 18th centuries. Many of them were added to in the French period or, more commonly, during the British Protectorate, and there are also a good many later buildings put up during the Protectorate which are often difficult to distinguish from the old. The buildings of this period are generally Italianate in style, embodying Renaissance and Baroque elements specially moulded and adapted to local conditions. Because of the lack of space and the density of the population, the building land was divided up into small lots and most of them were occupied by tall ur-

25. The front of the Giallinas mansion, one of the oldest of the aristocratic town houses in Corfu. Even after being redesigned and altered several times, it still has its striking vaulted porch. (Reconstruction by A. Agoropoulou-Birbili).

26. The facade of the Catholic Bishop's Palace. The building is now a branch of the National Bank of Greece. (Reconstraction by A. Agoropoulou-Birbili).

ban apartment blocks, which were packed closely together between the narrow streets. The windows and doors of these buildings were usually rectangular, very often surmounted by a semicircular tympanum. Variety and interest are added by the use of ground-floor arcades, wrought-iron grilles on the windows, staircase window-lights, balconies and chimneys of every shape and size. Finely-carved stone balconies, which are less common, are a mark of the superior houses. The mansions of the nobility are scattered about the town: there was never an exclusive "aristocratic quarter". Usually they were two-storey or three-storey town houses, though sometimes they too were multi-storey blocks. The nobles had to maintain a house in the town, but their main residences were on their country estates. The **Ricci Mansion** on Odos Moustoxydi is an example of such a mansion, its balcony, as we have seen, was used as the "stewards box" at jousting competitions during the Carnival. In its original form it only had a single storey above its six-arched portico, and the balustrade of the balcony would originally have been made of stone. The construction of this building displays a quality which is not altogether lacking even in the large apartment blocks.

Churches

The total number of churches on the island is very large, possibly as high as 800. Thirty-nine are still standing within the boundaries of the Venetian town, including the churches in the forts (the garrison church of St George in the Old Fort being post-Venetian, as we have seen). The predominant type is the wooden-roofed single-nave (or sometimes three-aisled) basilica with an *exonarthex* along two or three of its sides. A monumental façade and a richly decorated ceiling (the *ourania*) are among the characteristic features of the larger churches. Some churches have wall-paintings in the *exonarthex,* while the walls of the main part of the church are often covered with crimson or blue silk and hung with icons. The style of these churches was modelled on the Italian art and architecture of the period: the local craftsmen absorbed the spirit of the Baroque, often adapting it to the simpler needs of the context they were working in. From the 17th century onwards, painting was strongly influenced by Western stylistic trends. Panaghiotis Doxaras (1662-1729) studied in Rome and Venice, admired the great Venetian artists Tintoretto, Titian and Veronese and founded a school of painting on the Ionian Islands, making use of features that were quite new to the area and alien to the Byzantine tradition. The new style won many adherents on the Islands.

27. With a relatively large population to be accommodated in a confined space, multi-storey apartment blocks became the prevalent type of dwelling in Corfu town. The photograph shows a typical apartment block overlooking the Spianada.

The orientation of the churches in the town is quite arbitrary, owing to the lack of space. Most of the churches are squeezed between houses and some of them even have a house built over them. Belfries are a characteristic feature of the Corfu churches: some of them are Venetian-style campaniles, but on the later churches they are often simpler structures consisting of a fenestrated wall, tapering towards the top, with bells hanging in the apertures.

The most important town churches are described in the following paragraphs.

St Spyridon is without doubt the most famous church on the island. It was built in 1590 to replace an older church dedicated to the same Saint, which was located in Sarokko and was demolished to make way for the town walls. Its bell-tower resembles that of the Greek Orthodox church of St George in Venice, with which it is practically contemporary, and is the only interesting external feature of the church. The ceiling was painted by Panaghiotis Doxaras on seventeen cloth panels in 1727, but the gilt-scrolled frames bordering the panels are all that is left of the original decoration. The subjects of these paintings included miracles performed by St Spyridon, other scenes from his life and the four Evangelists. The Doxaras panels were greatly admired, but unfortunately they eventually rotted in the humid atmosphere and were replaced in the mid-19th century with copies of decidedly inferior quality by N. Aspiotis. The marble iconostasis and the elaborate reliquary (specially made in Vienna) containing the Saint's body, which is kept in a chapel to the right of the sanctuary, also date from the 19th century. St Spyridon, the island's patron saint, was a Cypriot bishop who took part in the first Ecumenical Council (A.D. 325). His body was kept in Constantinople until the fall of the city to the Turks in 1453, when it was brought to Corfu together with the remains of St Theodora (now in the Cathedral). The processions in which the Saint's body is carried round the town were instituted during the Venetian period and still take place four times a year. The oldest-established procession is the one held on Orthodox Holy Saturday to commemorate the Saint's miraculous intervention to save the island from a famine of unknown date. The procession of Palm Sunday and the first Sunday of November were inaugurated in memory of the island's deliverance from epidemics of the plague in 1629 and 1673, and that of 11th August to commemorate the repulse of the Turkish besiegers in 1716.

The Cathedral of the **Panaghia Spiliotissa** (Madonna of the Cave) is an imposing three-aisled basilica built in 1577. It stands high, at the head of a flight of steps, facing the harbour and the New Fort. Outstanding among the numerous icons in the Cathedral is one by Michael Damaskinos (16th century) of St George slaying the dragon, framed by ten scenes of the Saint's martyrdom. There are also several icons by Emmanuel Tzane Bounialis (17th century), the best of which is one of the martyr Gobdelas, on the left door of the iconostasis. The Last Supper by Panaghiotis Paramythiotis (18th century) is an example of the way Western iconographic types were sometimes used in Greek icon-painting.

The Campiello quarter contains four of the oldest churches on the island: the **Panaghia Antivouniotissa** was probably constructed in the 15th century. It is one of the wealthiest churches in the town. Many noblemen, identifiable by the coats of arms on their tombstones, lie buried in the *exonarthex* which runs round three sides of the church. There are two entrance doors on the north side, approached by a fine, broad flight of steps leading up from the seafront. Its fenestrated belfry is located on the north side of the church. The *exonarthex* bears traces of wall-paintings and the main part of the church is decorated with attractive icons of the Cretan school, the best ones being the *Noli Me Tangere* by Emmanuel Tzane Bounialis, St Alexios with scenes from his life by Stefanos Giancarolas and Christ Pantokrator (the Almighty) and the Panaghia Odigitria (Our Lady of Guidance) by Emmanuel Lombardos. The coffered ceiling is unpainted but decorated with gilt ornamentation.

The **Panaghia Kremasti,** built in the 16th century, is a church of the same type as the Panaghia Antivouniotissa but on a smaller scale. All that remains of the *exonarthex* is the west wing. The original ceiling has not survived, but there is a fine stone iconostasis and some huge Italianate icons by Spyros Speranzas (18th century), which are quite impressive. In front of the church is the most attractive square in the town, which is on two levels, with a beautifully sculptured well-head of the 16th century in the middle of the lower level.

Aghios Nikolaos ton Yerondon (St Nicholas of the Old Men) used to be one of the most important churches in the town, for it was the Cathedral of the Great Protopapas. Built in the early part of the 16th century, it has many similarities with the two previous churches, as well as differences which are due to the fact that the design has been adapted to the sloping ground of the site. An unusual feature is the pulpit, which stands against the north wall and is entered from the *exonarthex*. The paintings of St Theodora, St Kerkyra and Holy Communion on the doors of the iconostasis are attributed to Tzane. The exterior of the church has been considerably altered by renovation.

The **Church of the Pantokrator** (the Almighty) is simpler than the other three. Built during the second half of the 16th century, it was badly damaged by bombing in 1943, and has recently been restored. Its ceiling is undecorated. The 18th-century iconostasis was painted by George Chrysoloras. Some icons by Emmanuel Tzane Bounialis, taken from an older (17th-century) iconostasis, may also be seen here.

Other churches of interest in the town are the following:
Aghia Triada (the Holy Trinity), dating from the early 17th century.
Aghios Ioannis o Prodromos (St John the Baptist) built in the 16th century, which contains icons by Tzenos and Chrysoloras; Nikiphoros Theotokis, who served as a priest here for many years, preached from its pulpit. Nearby is the **Panaghia ton Xenon** (Our Lady of the Strangers), with a ceiling painted by N. Koutouzis (18th century). The Church of

Mandrakina is situated near the Old Fort, while **Limniotissa,** with a graceful bell-tower and a home built over the narthex, is in Campiello. The church of the **Proto Nekrotaphio** (First Cemetery), which was built in 1840 outside the boundaries of the Venetian town, used to contain a large collection of important paintings of the 16th and 17th centuries, including five signed works by Michael Damaskinos, some of which are now in the Collection of Christian Art in the Palace.

Of the Catholic churches, the most interesting are the **Cathedral of St James** (17th century), which gave its name to the nearby theatre of San Giacomo, the **Church of St Francis** and the Church of **Our Lady of Tenedos,** which is the most strikingly baroque building on the island. Finally, in Mandouki, there is the *Katholikon* of the **Platytera Monastery** (18th century), which was destroyed by the French in 1799 but restored immediately afterwards. It contains a variety of important 17th-century paintings, including a Madonna and Child by Emmanuel Tzane Bounialis, the Apocalypse by Theodore Poulakis, the Last Judgment by George Klodzas and two large paintings by N. Kandounis (the Washing of the Feet and the Last Supper) on the north and south walls. A beautifully-carved wooden iconostasis bears a series of Italianate icons by N. Koutouzis, a pupil of N. Kandounis (18th century). The tomb of Ioannis Kapodistrias may also be seen here.

One other monument of the Venetian period that must be mentioned is the marble **statue of Schulenburg,** which used to stand inside the Old Fort but was moved to its present position outside the gateway in the 19th century. The statue was carved out of Carrara marble by the Italian sculptor A. Corradini and shows the Count dressed in a Roman toga and breastplate, with a wig on his head and a laurel wreath on his brow. The Venetians erected the statue in the Count's lifetime as a token of their gratitude for the services he rendered them in 1716.

The 19th Century to 1864: the French and British

The French took a great interest in the appearance of the town. One of its most striking features is the arcaded pavement of the **Liston,** along the northern half of the west side of the Spianada. This row of houses was designed by the same French engineer, de Lesseps, who built an almost identical row on the Rue du Rivoli in Paris (his son was the designer of the Suez Canal). The arcade fits in perfectly with the architecture of the older buildings of the town. The French also planted trees on the Spianada

28. The north wall of the Church of the Panaghia Kremasti, showing the interesting geometrical designs of the plaster relief work. (A. Agoropoulou-Birbili).

29. The facade of the Church of the Panaghia Kremasti. In front of the church there is a picturesque piazza on two levels with a fine Venetian well-head.

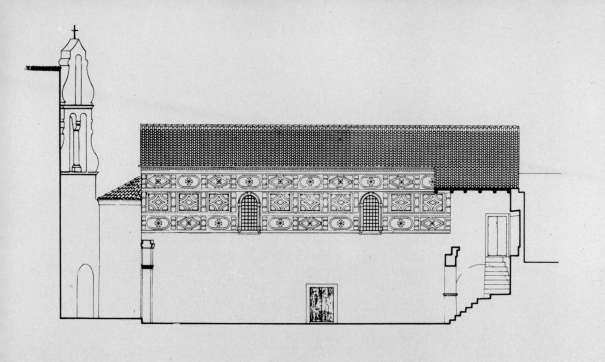

57

which was gradually transformed from an open expanse of wasteland into a centre of the town's social life and recreation.

The British have left their mark on the Spianada in particular, and on other parts of the town as well. Major construction work was done on the New Fort, though some of it was demolished in 1864 under the terms of the agreement for the union of Corfu with Greece (the neutrality of Corfu). The Fort is closed to the public, mainly to protect visitors from the dangers of falling masonry and getting lost in the labyrinth of passages and rooms. The British imposed order upon the chaotic building regulations, and the maximum building height was increased. An interesting building on the west side of the northern part of the Spianada is the clubhouse of the Corfu Literary Society, which founded in 1836 with the object of providing cultural (improvement) and leisure activities for its members. The Society has an excellent library specializing in books on the Ionian Islands, as well as collections of icons and paintings which it is hoped will shortly be put on public exhibition. The Prefecture, designed by the Corfiot architect Chronis, is a most attractive building erected in 1840 at the upper end of the Spianada. A plaque on the wall states that Ioannis Kapodistrias was born there (i.e. in an older building on the same site). The Ionian Parliament building, just above Odos Moustoxydi, is by the same architect: it was here that the Assembly voted for the union of the Ionian Islands with Greece. Later on it was used as Protestant Church. It was badly damaged in 1943, and the façade with its Doric columns is all that is left on the original building. The obelisk in honour of Sir Howard Douglas, at the beginning of the road to Garitsa, is another monument of this period.

It is on the Spianada that the British influence is most noticeable. Near the southeast corner there stands a **rotunda with Ionic columns,** which was erected in honour of Sir Thomas Maitland in 1816. A bronze statue of Sir Frederick Adam by the sculptor P. Prosalendis stands in front of the Palace, which commands the northern part of the esplanade: the Lord High Commissioner is shown standing, wearing a mantle and pointing with his left arm towards a small fountain, a gesture symbolising the construction of the town aqueduct. The statue was put up by the Ionian Government out of gratitude for the public works carried out under Adam's administration.

The most splendid edifice of the British period is the huge **neoclassical Palace** at the top end of the Spianada, which was built as the official residence of the Lords High Commissioners. Construction started in 1819 to a design by G. Whitmore, who succeeded in making it pleasantly imposing without being heavy, in spite of its size. It is built of stone from Malta, and its façade is embellished with a Doric colonnade and two entrance gateways with triumphal arches. The cornice is adorned with reliefs which are allegorical representations of the seven islands, Corfu being depicted as an ancient galley. Besides being the residence of the High Commissioner, the building was used as a meeting-place for the Ionian Senate and as the headquarters of the Order of St Michael and St George, which was instituted in 1818. From 1864 to 1913 it was used as the summer residence of the Greek royal family. It now houses a museum, the local offices of the Archaeological Service, the Archives of the island (which contain some very important documents that are sadly neglected) and the Public Library of 60,000 volumes. The coats of arms of the local nobility may be seen in the library anteroom.

The Town after the Union with Greece

A stroll along Odos Arseniou, the seafront road which runs along the top of the walls, is one of the pleasantest walks in the town, with a fine view towards Vido Island on one side and the attractive old houses on the other. One of these houses was the home of Dionysios Solomos, and here you may see a bust of the poet done between the wars by the sculptor M. Tombros. Continuing towards the Spianada with its interesting blend of styles from three different periods (the Venetian, the French and the British), it is worth going into the public gardens to look at Prosalendis' marble **statue of Lord Guilford,** who is shown sitting with an open book in his hands. Nearby there is a bust of L. Mavilis. The 19th-century marble **statue of Ioannis Kapodistrias,** which stands in the southwest corner of the Spianada, is too conspicuous to miss. It shows the first President standing in thought, wrapped in a long cape.

Outside the old town, where efforts are being made to preserve the existing buildings intact, there has been considerable expansion to the south and west, particularly in recent years. Apartment blocks, broad streets and massive hotels — especially the last — provide eloquent testimony to the island's development, which is largely due to tourism. Outside the town there is a very good network of roads, unusually extensive by Greek standards, which makes it easy to explore the beautiful countryside in comfort.

CORFU

_____ the Kanoni peninsula

_____ itinerary to Kassiopi, Roda and Sidari

_____ itinerary to Kavos

_____ itinerary to Paleokastritsa and Ermones

Sidari
Roda
Karousades
Strinillas
Kassiopi
Kouloura
Kalami
Spartillas
Nissaki
Aghios Markos
Barbati
Ipsos
Krini
Lakones
Gardelades
Dassia
Angelokastro
Paleokastritsa
Gouvia
Kontokali
CORFU
Analipsis
Mirtiotissa
Glifada
Perama
Sinarades
Achillion
Gastouri
Benitses
Aghios Mattheos
Morakika
Messongi
Gardiki
Chlomos
Petreti
Argirades
Lefkimmi
Kavos
Panaghia of Arkoudilla

A L B A N I A

TOUR OF THE ISLAND

The countryside of Corfu is as lovely as the town. The four itineraries proposed here will enable the visitor to cover most of the island and to visit all the best-known monuments and the most beautiful beaches, but the whole island is very beautiful and the sea crystal-clear and inviting all round its coast, so you need have no hesitation in leaving the beaten track and doing some exploring on your own. There is no danger of getting lost, and it is more than likely that you will have the satisfaction of discovering for yourself some remote monastery, picturesque little village or secluded cove where you can plunge into the sapphire and emerald sea.

THE KANONI PENINSULA

This is the shortest excursion to be made from the town, and until a few decades ago was also the most idyllic. Entire generations of Corfiots and visitors have walked or ridden in their carriages to Garitsa, to the hill of Analipsis or on to Kanoni, but the scenery has now been spoilt by the rapid spate of building construction in recent years. Massive buildings have risen where there used to be peaceful gardens and olivegroves, hiding the view of the sea. Here and there a few quiet corners have remained untouched as reminders of Paleopolis as it used to be.

The scant remains of ancient Korkyra (see chapter entitled "The Ancient City") were found on the Paleopolis peninsula. The Byzantine church of SS Jason and Sosipater is located just past Garitsa Bay in the suburb of Anemomilos. Some distance further on you will see the ruins of the Basilica of Aghia Kerkyra (Paleopolis Church) by the side of the road (see chapter on "Early Christian and Byzantine Monuments near the Town").

The hill of **Analipsis,** approximately 3 kilometres out of the town, is one of the most romantic and peaceful spots on the island. From here there is a fine view of the town, the Citadel, the coast of the mainland across the channel and a large part of the Mon Repos estate. The villa of **Mon Repos** was built in 1831 as the summer residence of the British Lord High Commissioner, Sir Frederick Adam, and later it became the

Analipsis

Mon Repos

61

property of the Greek royal family. Even after the abolition of the monarchy in Greece, Mon Repos is still closed to the public.

Kardaki

A small path leads down from the hill of Analipsis to **Kardaki,** a small murmuring spring near the sea, buried deep among the shrubs and flowers. According to a local legend, used by Lorenzos Mavilis in one of his poems, he who drinks water from this fountain will never return to his native land.

Kanoni

Kanoni, with its view of the "trade-mark" of Corfu, is the high point of this excursion, for it is still one of the most picturesque beauty-spots in Greece in spite of the rapid tourist development of recent years. The hotels and noisy coaches intrude, certainly, but they have not succeeded in destroying the fragile grace of the landscape and the subtle nuances of colour on the water at sunset, nor do they totally overwhelm the human dimension. There are two islets just offshore. The nearer of the two, which is just large enough for the Convent and Church of Vlachernon, is joined to the mainland by a

Pondikonissi

narrow causeway. The other, **Pondikonissi** or Mouse Island, is a densely vegetated islet which is one of the many "petrified ships" of local legend. This, too, has a church on it, dedicated to Christ the Pantokrator (11th or 12th century).

Perama

A narrow causeway, for pedestrians and cyclists only, connects Kanoni with **Perama,** which faces it across the mouth of the Chalikiopoulos Lagoon.

ITINERARY TO KASSIOPI, RODA AND SIDARI

This itinerary covers the north-east and north-west parts of this island. For most of the way the road runs along the shore, providing plenty of opportunities for bathing from the coves and beaches, some of them popular and usually crowded — such as Dassia, Ipsos and Sidari — and others secluded and peaceful. The inland route to Sidari is one of the loveliest drives on the island.

Gouvia

On leaving the town, the road passes through the village of Kondokali (5km) and continues towards the north. On **Gouvia** Bay the ruins of the Venetian naval arsenal bear witness to the old, glorious days of the Venetian fleet, when the galleys of the Serene Republic dominated the sea-routes to the East. After the village of Gouvia a road off to the left leads to the Castello Hotel, built by the Italian Mimbelli. It is a reproduction of a Venetian palazzo 14th-century, and with its large rooms, wood panelling and decorative wood-carving it succeeds very well in capturing the period atmosphere.

THE KANONI
PENINSULA

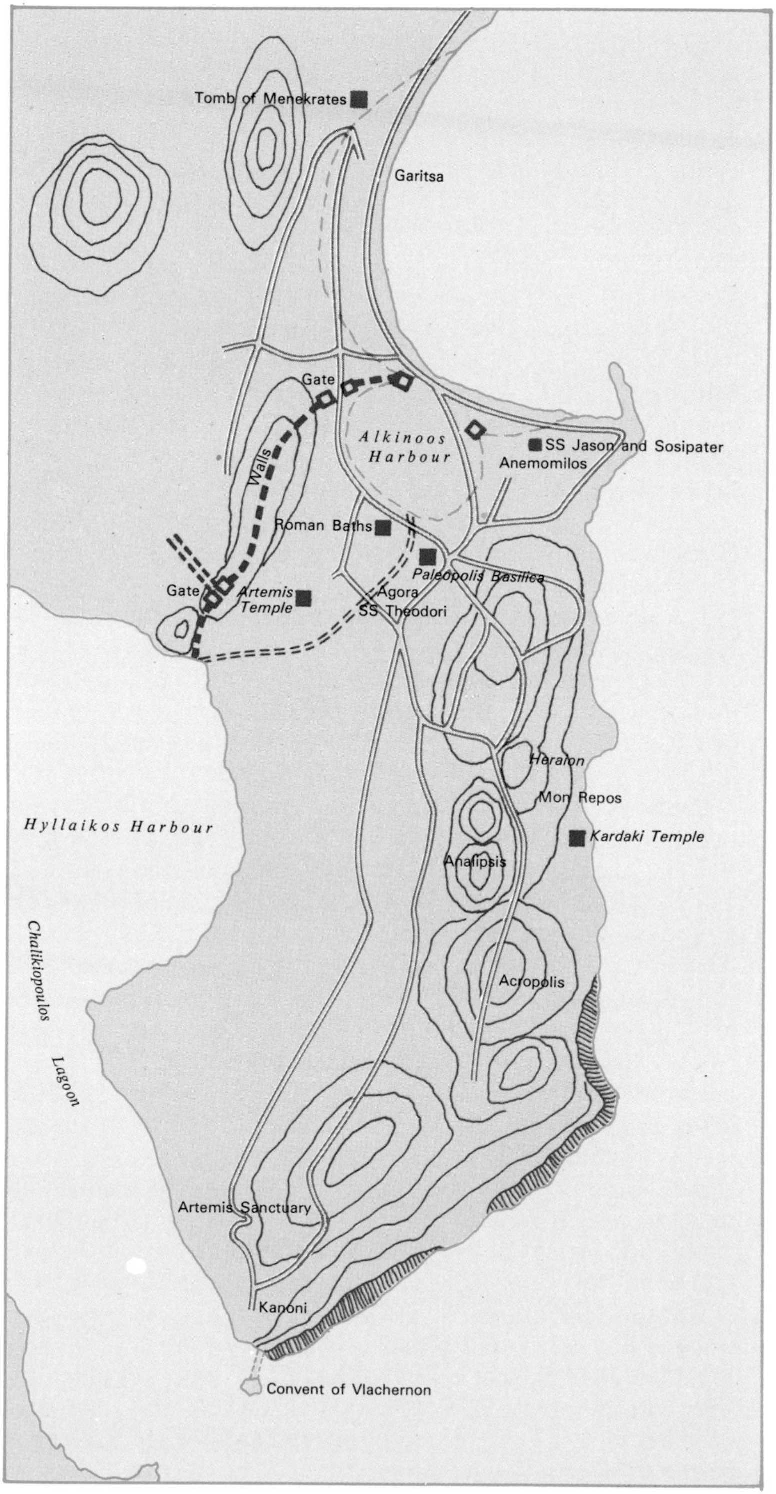

Tomb of Menekrates

Garitsa

Gate

Alkinoos
Harbour

Walls

SS Jason and Sosipater
Anemomilos

Roman Baths

Paleopolis Basilica

Gate

Artemis
Temple

Agora

SS Theodori

Heraion

Mon Repos

Hyllaikos Harbour

Kardaki Temple

Analipsis

Chalikiopoulos

Acropolis

Lagoon

Artemis Sanctuary

Kanoni

Convent of Vlachernon

The turning to the right at the same crossroads takes you to
Dassia beach (13 km), a popular, colourful holiday resort with
luxuriant vegetation, hotels and restaurants and a wide variety
of sports and recreational facilities. The Polynesian straw huts
of the Club Méditerrannée are perhaps the most striking
feature of this stretch of coastline. The next bay, that of **Ipsos**
(15 km), with its narrow shingle beach, is the second-biggest
seaside resort after Dassia. It is dominated by the wooded
slopes of Mount Pantokrator, Corfu's highest mountain, which
towers majestically over it. At the end of the bay, just after the
hamlet of Pyrgi, take the left fork to the village of **Aghios
Markos** (less than 2 km from the turning), where there are two
interesting churches: in the village there is the Church of the
Pantokrator, with frescoes of 1576 in an excellent state of
preservation, and a short distance away is the Church of
Aghios Merkourios, the most important Byzantine monument
of the island after the Church of SS Jason and Sosipater, with
frescoes dating from 1075.

Return from here to the main road and continue towards
Kassiopi. Another turning to the left, 3 km after Ipsos, leads to
the villages of **Spartillas** and **Strinillas,** which are built on the
mountainside with a lovely view over the sea. The road is bad
and the ascent difficult, but the variety of the scenery and the
panoramic view from the top are unbelievably beautiful. From
Strinillas a rough road continues to the summit of **Mount Pantokrator.** From the top you can see the coast of Epiros and
Albania, Lake Butrinto, the small islands of Othoni, Erikousa
and Mathraki to the north-west of Corfu, the hills of Lefkimmi
in the south, the island of Paxi and, in the far distance,
Kefallonia. The Monastery of the Pantokrator is located on the
site of an older Angevin monastery which was built in 1347
and destroyed early in the 16th century. It was then completely
rebuilt, starting in 1689, with the help of contributions from the
people of the surrounding villages. There is practically nothing
left of the older monastery. The façade of the church was built
in the 19th century.

Returning to the main route, turn left along the Kassiopi
road, which skirts the eastern flanks of Mount Pantokrator
about 200 metres above the sea. If you take any of the paths
that wind down through the olives and cypresses, you can dis-
cover some of the most attractive coves on the island; one
track leads down to **Barbati,** a wide bay with a long sandy
beach. A little further on is **Nissaki** (22 km), a popular resort
with considerable tourist development, where good bathing is
off the rocks. In summer there is a regular boat service between
here and Corfu town. After the villages of Kendroma and

Dassia

Ipsos

Aghios Markos

Spartillas
Strinillas

Mount Pantokrator

Barbati
Nissaki

Gimari, take the turning to the right which leads to **Kouloura,**
a small fishing village with a Venetian fortified manor-house.
The small twin cove of **Kalami** has been made famous by
Lawrence Durrell's descriptions of it in *Prospero's Cell.* The
"small white house" may still be seen today, and neither the
appearance of the village nor the way of life has changed much
since the days when Durrell lived and wrote there. All along
this stretch of road there is a good view of Albania: the channel
separating it from Corfu is only 1 1/2 miles wide. After
Kouloura the road leaves the coast and strikes inland.

    Kassiopi (36 km), a small town at the north-east corner of
the island, is connected with Corfu town by a daily boat service. Practically nothing remains of the flourishing Roman
town of Cassiope (the Emperor Nero visited it and sang at the
altar of Jupiter Cassius), but the ruins of the Angevin fortress,
which was one of the island's main strongholds, are still
standing. The Church of the Panaghia Kassopitissa (Our Lady
of Kassiopi) now stands on the site of the Temple of Jupiter. In
the middle ages it was the most venerated church on the island,
and ships passing trough the channel used to fire a one-gun
salute in its honour. The Turks looted it twice and it was rebuilt
in 1590, as we learn from a Latin inscription over the north
door. The church contains an icon of the Madonna and Child
by Th. Poulakis (17th century). Nowadays Kassiopi is a popular holiday resort with many shops, restaurants and hotels.

    Beyond Kassiopi the road continues along the north coast of
the island and the scenery changes: here you are in a landscape
of barren, rocky hills. After passing the Andinioti Lagoon you
come eventually to **Roda,** a small village on a vast sandy
beach. A temple of the 5th century B.C. has been discovered
here, and some architectural fragments from it may be seen in
the Corfu Archaelogical Museum. Although the area is mainly
agricultural, the tourist boom has reached here in recent years
and hotels and restaurants have started springing up.

    From Roda take the road to **Karoussades,** a picturesque
village where the main point of interest is the mansion of the
long-established Theotokis family, who came to Corfu from
Constantinople. The oldest parts of this fortified manor-house
were probably built in the 15th century. The road from
Karoussades to **Sidari** (5 km) is macadamised (a new road was
under construction in 1979). Sidari is a small village on an ex-
ceptionally lovely sandy beach. At one point on the coast
nearby there are some unusual formations of soft rock rising
out of the sea, forming a channel which is called the Canal
d'Amour. In many places the banks of the channel have been
eroded and fallen into the sea, but the place has not lost its

charm. (According to local tradition, any girl who swims the whole length of the channel will receive her heart's desire, but few are bold enough to make the attempt).

From Sidari take the road to the south. The drive from Sidari to Arkadades is one of the most attractive on the island. The road passes through tall ferns and shrubs and is shaded by olive trees and cypresses. Modern life does not seem to have penetrated here. The women still wear their local costumes while riding on heavily laden donkeys, and the colourful villages and old Venetian farms have remained unchanged with the passage of time. In Arkadades fork right for Pagi (6km), beyond which a macadam road continues for a further 4 km through the finest olive groves on the island, to reach the sea at **Aghios Georgios.** The beach at Aghios Georgios is enchanting, certainly one of the most beautiful on the island: practically deserted and at least five kilometres in length, it is protected on one side by the gentle, wooded hills where the dark green of cypresses is mingled with the silvery grey of the olive trees.

Aghios Georgios

Take the main road back to Corfu town over the **Troumbetta Pass,** from where there is a panoramic view over the interior of the island, with its low hills and olive groves. The town is visible in the middle distance. A few kilometres after the picturesque village of **Skripero** you join the main road from Paleokastritsa to Corfu.

Troumbetta Pass

Skripero

ITINERARY TO KAVOS

This route takes you to the southernmost part of the island by way of the stretch of coast between Perama and Benitses which is sometimes known as the *"Côte d'Azur"* of Corfu, with all its holiday villas and hotels. There is something for everybody on this itinerary: interesting monuments, picturesques villages set amidst wonderfully varied vegetation, and beaches which are not too crowded. The main tourist attraction is the Achillion.

Leave the town by the road past the airport and continue towards Aghios Mattheos and Sinarades. From Sinarades a road descends to **Aghios Gordis** (16 km), which is one of the most beautiful beaches within easy reach of the town. Some large hotels have recently been built here, next to the small seaside restaurants.

Aghios Gordis

Retrace your steps to the main road, turn right towards the Achillion and you come soon to Gastouri (10 km), one of the best-known villages of Corfu. From here the road climbs through a leafy paradise of geraniums and cypresses, olive trees and bougainvillaeas to the **Achillion,** the palace built for Elisabeth of Austria. The biographers of the "melancoly empress" record that, after a few brief visits to Corfu, Elisabeth decided in 1890 to build a country seat there in honour of Achilles and Thetis, a place where she could get away from the intrigues and clamour of the Hapsburg court. The result, however, is not in the least like what one thinks of as a retreat. The Achillion is a pretentious, over-ornate building in the neoclassical style, completely out of keeping with its surroundings. The huge gardens are its most pleasing feature. The not unattractive second-floor veranda with the Ionic peristyle houses some bad sculptures: busts of ancient philosophers, of Shakespeare and of the nine Muses. The statue of the dying Achilles in the garden, by the German scylptor Herter, is the best in the Achillion. Further on is a huge statue of Achilles triumphant standing 8 metres high, a bad piece of work badly placed, since it cannot be seen properly from anywhere. The view from this point, however, provides ample compensation: below you are the Chalikiopoulos Lagoon, Kanoni, Pondikonissi and Perama, and in the distance Mount Pantokrator. The melancoly Elisabeth used to come here to watch the sunrise. Among the other sculptures in the gardens are statues of Phryne, Lord Byron and the Empress herself.

Downstairs there is a series of rooms decorated in Pompeian style, containing personal momentoes of the Empress. Just inside the front door, on the right, is a chapel with frescoes on the walls.

After Elisabeth's assassination by the Italian anarchist Luzzeni in Geneva, Kaiser Wilhelm II of Germany bought the palace and often spent his summers there. Nowadays most visitors go to his study on the first floor to have a look at the saddle which the eccentric emperor had fitted to his desk chair. The Achillion has recently been converted into a casino, which has brought new life and a different atmosphere to the "mournful" palace.

Leaving the Achillion, go down the hill to join the coast road from Perama to Moraitika. **Benitses** (12 km) is a fishing village **Benitses** which is now a crowded holiday resort, set amidst lemon and orange groves. Here you can see the ruins of a Roman villa of the 3rd century A.D. and of a Roman bath-house. At **Moraitika** **Moraitika** (20 km) there are some huge new tourist hotels. The remains of a Roman villa were found outside the village, and so it seems that Corfu was a popular place for seaside holidays even in antiquity, just as it is today.

Two kilometres beyond Moraitika one take the right turning towards the village of Mesonghi and the bridge over the

Aghios Mattheos

Gardiki

Chlomos

Aghios Georgios

Lefkimmi

Kavos

Mesonghi River. From the Mesonghi bridge it is about 5 km to **Aghios Mattheos,** one of the biggest villages on the island, surrounded by a large forest of oak and olive trees which stretches high up hillside towards the Pantokrator Monastery. There is a deep cave near the monastery, from which there is said to be an underground passage leading down to the sea; be that as it may, it is certainly true that you can faintly hear the sound of the waves from inside the cave. Before you reach the village there is a track off to the left leading to the impressive Byzantine fort of **Gardiki** (about 1 km), standing on a low hill. This consists of an octagonal circuit-wall with eight strong towers, some of which have decorative courses of tiles. A number of architectural members from ancient buildings, possibly from a fountain-house, have been used in the construction of the fort, which dates from the 13th century.

Return to the main road, which you rejoin near the Mesonghi bridge, and turn south. At Linia (9.5 km) there is a road to the right leading to Lake Koryssia, which is actually a lagoon because there is a narrow channel connecting it with the sea. Five kilometres off to the left from Linia is **Chlomos,** an attractive hill village with some old houses. Three kilometres beyond Linia there is another turning to the right, taking you down to the west coast of **Aghios Georgios** (4 km), where there is a long sandy beach. Continuing along the road to Kavos, you pass through Arghirades, where there is a turning on the left to Petreti (3 km), a small, picturesque fishing village. Then on through **Lefkimmi** (39 km), the biggest town in southern Corfu, to Kavos (74 km), situated on a long beach backed by groves of olives and cypresses. Tourist development has come to **Kavos** in recent years. In summer there is a regular boat service from Corfu town, and the passenger ferry that plies between Corfu and Paxi in the summer also calls here. Three kilometres further south is the small fortified Monastery of the Panaghia Arkoudillas, in a beautiful setting of luxuriant foliage near Cape Asprokavos.

ITINERARY TO PALEOKASTRITSA AND ERMONES

The best-known seaside resort on Corfu, which has been the most popular beauty-spot on the island ever since the British occupation of last century, is Paleokastritsa. In spite of the coachloads of tourists pouring in from the town, in spite of the restaurants and hotels and the heavy tourist development, the natural beauty of the landscapé still retains its powerful charm and appeal.

Leave Corfu town by the road to the north and follow the signs to Paleokastritsa. **Paleokastritsa** (25 km), a place of pretty coves reparated by precipitous headlands, has been identified by some scholars with the site of Alkinoos' palace. The offshore rock of Kolovri is traditionally held to be the petrified ship of Odysseus; or, according to an alternative story, it is the ship of an Algerian corsair who was sailing in to loot the monastery, which was turned to stone on the spot in answer to the Abbot's prayers.

The six coves of Paleokastritsa are named Aghia Triada, Platakia, Alipa, Aghios Spyridon, Aghios Petros and Ambelaki. The first three form a cluster in the shape of a cloverleaf. Paleokastritsa today is a crowded and noisy resort. Practically every visitor to the island goes there at least once, attracted either by its fame as a beauty-spot or by the facilities for water-sports and fishing, or else to try some lobster, the local speciality.

The Monastery of Paleokastritsa was founded in 1225. The present building, which dates from the 18th and 19th centuries, is an interesting example of a monastery with an arcaded cloister-garth. A small museum houses an interesting collection of Byzantine and post-Byzantine icons.

Leave Paleokastritsa by the same road, and after a few kilometres you come to a left turning which leads to the village of Lakones (4 km from the main road) and **Bella Vista** (6 km), a vantage-point just beyond the village from which there is a panoramic view of Paleokastritsa with its deeply-indented blue coves. It has been said that the view from Bella Vista is one of the finest anywhere in the Mediterranean. Distance softens the impact of the modern tourist developments, and from here you can appreciate the extraordinary beauty of Paleokastritsa without being bothered by the noise of coaches and speed-boats.

Beyond Bella Vista the road continues the village of Krini, from where it is a three-kilometre walk to the scant remains of **Angelokastro,** one of the Byzantine forts on the island. It was built by Michael Angelos I, Despot of Epiros. The town of Corfu is visible from the hilltop and the local garrison could signal the approach of enemy vessels.

Return from here to the main Paleokastritsa-Corfu road. After a few kilometres turn right towards Gardelades and before reaching the village you come out on to the main road along the Ropa valley, which brings you to the coast again at **Ermones,** another well-known seaside resort. Some scholars maintain that it was here that Odysseus met Nausikaa when she and her handmaidens were washing their linen in the

Paleokastritsa

Bella Vista

Angelokastro

Ermones

stream and spreading it out on the pebbles of the beach to dry. Nowadays Ermones is a beach with ice-cold water, precipitous cliffs and an extremely large hotel built on the rocky hillside.

Mirtiotissa South of Ermones there are two more magnificent beaches at **Mirtiotissa** and Glifada. The first can only be reached on foot, from a crossroads on the road from Pelekas to Vatos. This is undoubtedly the most beautiful beach on Corfu: remote and totally secluded, with shallow, crystal-clear water and little streamlets trickling down into the sea over the rocks at either end of the beach. The sense of solitude in absolute. The Monastery of Mitriotissa (Our Lady of the Myrtles), said to have been founded in the 14th century by a Turk who was converted to Christianity, is beautifully positioned in a setting of cypresses, olive trees and banana trees (the only ones on the island).

Glifada **Glifada** (17 km from the town) is a long sandy beach with pellucid, shallow water; it has recently been developed into a major holiday resort.

Pelekas The road back to the town takes you through the village of **Pelekas.** Kaiser Wilhelm II used to watch the sunset from a hill outside the village, which has been known since then as the Kaiser's Throne. From this spot you can see across the island to Corfu town in the east, then let your eye sweep round over the olive groves to the north and out over the Ionian Sea to the west: the sight of the sun sinking majestically to rest in the evening is one you will never forget.

30. The Old Fort from the Spianada. 30

31. The Serene Republic employed some of the best Venetian architects and engineers on the fortifications of Corfu town, which were built in several phases over a period of four hundred years. Their first task was the construction of the

33

Old Fort on the site of the old Byzantine citadel. This photograph gives a general view of the Old Fort.

32. The Old Fort from the north.   *33. The south side of the Old Fort.*

34

34. *One of the projects carried out by the Venetians to strengthen Corfu's defences in the 16th century was the enlargement of the Spianada or esplanade, i.e. the open space between the citadel (the Old Fort) and the xopoli (the part of the town that lay outside the citadel walls). The creation of the Spianada had a decisive effect on the subsequent layout of the town. This view of the Spianada, with the town in the background, is taken from the Old Fort (some of its bastions are visible in the picture).*

35. *Part of the Savorgnan bastion (16th cent.), the Spianada and Garitsa Bay, seen from the Old Fort.* ▶

36. *The view from the Old Fort looking towards the Mourayia (the sea walls on the north side of the citadel).*

35

37. The main gate of the Old Fort. The original drawbridge over the Contrafossa (moat) has been replaced by a fixed iron bridge 60 metres long.

38. The Contrafossa — the moat dug by the Venetians across the neck of the fortified promontory — turned the Old Fort into an artificial island.

39

39. The vast expanse of the Spianada was landscaped by the French and British, who took pains to improve the appearance of the town. Once it had been planted with trees by the French, it ceased to be an esplanade in the military sense of the term and started being used by the townspeople as a place for social gatherings and outdoor recreation.

40. At the north end of the Spianada, in front of the Palace stands the bronze statue of Sir Frederick Adam. The pool symbolizes the town aqueduct, one of the public work projects put in hand by Adam during his term of office.

*41, 42. The distinctive charm of Corfu town is made up of a wide variety of disparate elements, such as the contrast between the spacious breadth of the Spianada or the Garitsa seafront boulevard and the narrow **kandounia** (streets) of the crowded old town. At every turn the old rubs shoulders with the new, as in this picture of a horse-drawn carriage in front of a modern luxury hotel.*

41

43. *The colonnade along the front of the Palace.*

44. *The imposing Palace of St. Michael and St. George was built in the early years of the British Protectorate as the official residence of the Lords High Commissioners. The cornice is adorned with allegorical reliefs symbolizing the seven Ionian Islands.*

45. *St. George's Gate at the NE. end of the Spianada.*

45

44

46. *The **volta** («vaults») at the Liston. These famous arcades facing the Spianada are a legacy of the French occupation of Corfu. They were designed by Lesseps, the architect of the almost identical arcades in the Rue de Rivoli, Paris.*

47. *A Venetian well-head in the Spianada. In the background is the Palace of St Michael and St George.*

48. *The Ionic rotunda on the Spianada, erected in honour of Sir Thomas Maitland (Lord High Commissioner, 1816-1824).*

46

47

48

49. The New Fort was built by the Venetians in 1576, shortly after the town had successfully resisted the second Turkish siege. It was linked with the Old Fort by the west wall of the town. The town wall was completed in 1588. In the 19th century the British constructed a number of important new buildings in the New Fort.

50. The harbour — the hub of Corfu's maritime communications with the outside world — is situated at the foot of the hill on which the New Fort stands.

51, 52. Two views of Corfu harbour. ▶

51

53. The church of St Spyridon, Corfu's patron saint, was built in 1590 to replace an earlier church in the Sarokko quarter, which had to be demolished to make way for the fortification works of the 16th century.

54, 55. Four annual processions in honour of St Spyridon, in which the saint's reliques are carried through the streets of the town, were instituted during the Venetian period and are still held every year. They commemorate the island's deliverance from a famine, epidemics of the plague and the last Turkish assault, all of which were attributed to St Spyridon's miraculous intervention.

56. *This attractive, elegant building of 1840 now houses the offices of the Prefecture. Ioannis Kapodistrias was born in the house which previously stood on this site.*

57. *Corfu's present Town Hall, built in the 17th century, was originally the* **Loggia dei Nobili.** *After a short time it was converted into a theatre, and from the end of the 18th century it was used as an opera house.*

58. *The 17th-century church of Ayios Iakovos (San Giacomo) used to be the cathedral of the Catholics. It is in the most central square of the old town, next to the old theatre (now the Town Hall), which took its name from this church.*

57

58

59. Narrow streets of tall apartment buildings (many of them built in the 17th and 18th centuries, though subsequently altered) give Corfu its unique character. The town was forced to grow upwards because of the limited space available within the walls.

60. A fine 19th century building houses the library and collections of the Corfu Reading Society.

61. Tall campaniles of varied design are one of the distinctive features of Corfu town. This one is modelled on a Venetian original.

62. *One of the most attractive places in the town, combining fine architecture with a magnificent view, north of the Spianada.*

63. *The tall old buildings along Arseniou street, over the waterfront, look across to the small island of Vido and the mountains of Epiros across the strait.*

◄ *64. A view that never palls: the two islets off the southernmost point of the Kanoni peninsula, with Perama in the background.*

65. Nestling amidst verdant trees and shrubs on the islet of Pondikonissi (Mouse Island) stands the church of the Pantokrator (11th or 12th cent.).

66. The Vlacherna Convent covers almost all of the nearer islet, just a stone's throw from Kanoni.

67, 68. The Achillion, built on one of the most beatiful sites in the whole island, is surrounded by lovely gardens.

69. *Dassia on the east coast, north of the town, is situated in a setting of lush vegetation.*

70. *Ayios Gordios, commonly known as Ai-Gordis, is one of the most beautiful places on the west coast of Corfu.*

69

71, 72, 73. *On Gouvia Bay, a little way out of the town to the north, stands the old Venetian arsenal, a reminder of the days when Venice was at the peak of her glory.*

71

72

73

74. *Club Méditerranée holidaymakers at Dassia find plenty of opportunities to escape from the humdrum routine of everyday life.*

75. *Nissaki, one of the loveliest places on the east coast, may be reached in summer by caique from Corfu town.*

76, 77. Kassiopi is a popular holiday resort served by frequent boats to and from Corfu town.

78. *Kouloura, a small fishing harbour.*

79, 80, 81. Sidari, in the north of the island, with its extraordinary detached rocks thrusting up out of the sea and its magnificent beach, is a photographer's paradise.

CORRIGENDA

p. 29 Caption n. 13 refers to the lower picture, n. 14 to the upper one.

p. 42 line 14; instead of odos Menekratous read odos Kyprou. Caption n. 22, instead of facade read west face.

p. 45 line 5; instead of Garitsa read Anemomilos.

p. 46 line 24; instead of Michael Damaskinos read Emmanuel Tzanes.

p. 62 line 4 from the bottom; instead of built read it belonged.

p. 94 Caption 56, instead of now houses read housed the offices of the Prefecture up until 1967.

p. 106 Caption 69; instead of Dassia read Ipsos.

p. 128 The Sino-Japanese Museum has been recently renamed Museum of Asiatic Art.

p. 128 line 21; instead of 30 read 50
line 22; instead of 200 read 500.

p. 129 line 23; instead of Ya-yoi period (250B.C.-A.D.250) read the Jomon and Ya-yoi periods.

p. 129 line 37; instead of St Gabriel read St George.

p. 130 line 19; The sculptures of Gandhara are in room M.

p. 148 Caption 110, 111; line 21; add the first, K'ang Hsi (1662-1722) the second.

80

81

82, 83, 84. The charms of Paleokastritsa, on the west coast, have been sung by a host of admirers ever since it was "discovered" by travellers in the 19th century.

85. At Paleokastritsa, possibly more than anywhere else, the eye is ▶ immediately struck by the contrast between the green of the vegetation and the deep blue of the sea.

84

2

3

86, 87. Paleokastritsa Monastery (18th-19th cent.). is of architectural interest and stands in a superb position.

*88. Glyfada, on the west coast, has a long sandy beach and comfortable
hotel accommodation.*

89. Breathtaking is the sunset in the Ionian Sea.

THE MUSEUMS

THE ARCHAEOLOGICAL MUSEUM

This museum, which was opened about ten years ago, was built with the primary object of providing premises where the sculptures from the Temple of Artemis could be displayed to their best advantage, and the other local archaeological finds which had previously been kept in the Palace (at the north end of the Spianada) were moved here at the same time. The most interesting exhibits are described below in the order in which they are seen. It is worth stopping on the first-floor landing, before entering the corridor off to the left which leads to the Gorgon Room, to see three funerary monuments from the cemetery of the ancient city in Garitsa: a large burial pithos (6th century B.C.); the capital of a column (1st half of the 6th century B.C.) which used to stand on the tomb of one Menecrates, an the inscription informs us; and a funerary stele with inscription in Homeric hexameters extolling the heroism of a certain Arniadas, who lost his life in battle. The showcase on the landing contains Corinthian pottery from graves of the 7th and 6th centuries B.C.

The first room off the landing to the left contains a variety of small finds. The most interesting are the prehistoric artefacts in the first showcase on the left, which include Early Neolithic sherds from Sidari (6000 B.C.) and Bronze Age flints, implements and pots. The two showcases to the right of the entrance contain Corinthian pottery and Corcyraean imitations (7th and 6th centuries B.C.), mostly from graves in Garitsa. The lead tablets in the next showcase (late 6th and early 5th centuries B.C.), which come from excavations in the ancient city, are inscribed with records of debts. The outstanding exhibit in the showcase of terracotta figurines and statuettes is a fragment of a vase depicting the Judgment of Paris in relief. Of the architectural fragments on the wall, the best are the pieces from the roof of the Temple of Rhoda (5th century B.C.). Then we come to bronze statuettes, including one of a naked warrior and one of a woman wearing a peplos — both belonging to the Classical period (5th century B.C.) — together with a few Attic black-figure vases and some Laconian pottery. Two showcases on the opposite side of the room contain coins found on Corfu, notable among them being a silver coin showing a cow suckling her calf, which was minted by Corcyra when it became independent of its mother-city, Corinth. Later on, coins with different designs were circulated concurrently with these: some had an amphora on them, some had Pegasos on the obverse and Athena on the reverse, and so on. On the same side of the room there is a fine Corinthian *olpe* (jug) decorated with a variety of real and imaginary animals arranged in four horizontal bands, and an Attic black-figure *louterion* with two majestic lions depicted on it (6th century B.C.).

The next room, known as the Gorgon Room, is dominated by the huge Gorgon pediment from the Temple of Artemis, which is contemporary with the temple itself (590-580 B.C.). It is the western pediment and the oldest large stone pediment extant. The size alone of this imposing piece of work — 17 metres wide by a little over 3 metres high — is enough to show how bold was the vision of the Corinthian artist who designed it at a time when monumental sculpture was just beginning. When one compares the size of this project and the simplicity and variety of its component figures with the miniaturistic approach and love of detail apparent in other Corinthian work — vases especially — of about the same date, one can get some idea of the zestfulness and vitality characteristic of this period and the spirit of adventure reflected in this piece. The Gorgon is the central figure of the pediment. According to myth she was decapitated by Perseus — who did not make the mistake of looking directly at her and thus being turned to stone - and her two children, Pegasus and Chrysaor, sprang from her blood. Regardless of the myth (which the artist was familiar with, and which he knew his public was familiar with too, so he did not have to retell it), Pegasus is placed on the right of the Gorgon (as you look at the pediment) and Chrysaor on the left. The Gorgon is depicted running towards the right, with her knees bent in accordance with the stylistic convention of Archaic art, but with her torso and head turned full-face towards the spectator. She had to inspire a feeling of dread, and so she has been given monstrous features: teeth, tongue, snakes, wings etc. Pegasus, the winged horse that was the emblem of Corinth, had his forefeet resting on the Gorgon's arm, but there is hardly anything of him left. Chrysaor was holding a sword, now lost, and his face — one of the most beautiful in early Archaic art — is lit by a tender "archaic smile". The centrepiece is flanked by two fabulous creatures of the cat family: they are known as "leopanthers" because they have the head of a lion and the body of a panther, with their spotted markings represented by sets of concentric circles. Their heads are turned full-face towards the spectator. Their presence seems to ascribe to the Gorgon the attributes of the great Nature Goddess, attributes which Artemis, to whom the temple was dedicated, had inherited from prehistoric religions: Homer calls her *Potnia theron* (Mistress of beasts). Thus the implied presence of Artemis is combined with the terrible features of the Gorgon which serve an apotropaic purpose - in other words they help to ward off the evil influences of the powers of darkness. The remaining figures which the sculptor put in to fill the bottom corners of the triangular pediment are, of necessity, much smaller. On the right there is a scene from the *Titanomachy* (the war between the Olympian gods and the Titans), which resulted in the overthrow of the old gods (the Titans) by the new ones (the Olympians); here Zeus is depicted as a beardless young man striking a Titan with a thunderbolt. To the left, a seated figure extends an arm imploringly towards another person who is standing over the first with spear poised menacingly. This scene is most probably connected with the one on the right: it is thought to represent Rhea or Kronos being threatened by Poseidon, but an alternative conjecture is that the seated figure is Priam, who claimed sanctuary at the altar of Zeus after the fall of Troy, and that his attacker is the young Neoptolemos. This is the earliest instance of narrative scenes from mythology being depicted on an Archaic pediment. Both the corners were filled with reclining Titans, but the one on the right has been destroyed. The whole composition would originally have been painted in bright colours, like all Archaic sculpture, and it must have been even more impressive then than it is now.

Various other architectural fragments, some from the same temple and some from smaller buildings in the same sanctuary, are on exhibit in the same room. To the left of the entrance there is a restored section of the entablature of this Doric temple: the architrave and the frieze with its triglyphs and metopes. Fragments of the decorated sima of its original tiled roof may be seen further along the wall on the left, while on the opposite wall there are fragments of the marble roofing-slabs which replaced the original tiles c. 530 B.C. A fragment of a relief from the same temple, probably from the frieze, is thought to represent Memnon duelling with Achilles (who has unfortunately been destroyed). On your left as you go towards the next room is a small pediment (200 B.C.) which was part of a votive monument in the sanctuary of Artemis (200 B.C.). Another pediment which has recently been put on display in the next room is the museum's latest acquisition and an extremely important exhibit. It is the left half of a pediment dating from the Archaic period (c. 500 B.C.), which was found at Figareto on the road to Kanoni. It is in the next room after the Gorgon Room, facing the door so that it is the first thing you see as you walk in. The statuary gives a lively picture of a Dionysiac symposium, or drinking-party: two men are shown reclining on a couch, both looking at something in the right-hand part of the pediment, which has been lost. The elder of the two is the wine-god Dionysos, the other a youth holding a *kylix* (goblet) in his hand. The space in front of the couch is occupied by a small table and a reclining lion, while in the left-hand corner of the pediment there is a *krater* (mixing-bowl) of Laconian type with a large dog next to it.

Most of the exhibits in the next room come from excavations in the grounds of Mon Repos. The first objects that catch the eye are the architectural fragment from the great Temple of Hera, and especially the striking antefixes in the form of lions' heads, women's faces and gorgoneions (late 7th century B.C.) and one disc-shaped antefix with a painted rosette. Then there are two fine 6th-century votive offerings from the sanctuary, both standing on pedestals: one, which comes from a Laconian workshop, is a bronze statuette of a young reveller which probably adorned the rim of a large cauldron; the other, a small head of a kouros, is a graceful piece of Corinthian work (530 B.C.). The showcases contain a large collection of interesting finds, notably a terracotta quadriga with its charioteer and a charming little piglet in case II, a terracotta mask of a man in case 12 and a small Corinthian bronze horse (late 8th century B.C.), one of the earliest votive offerings in the sanctuary) and a beautiful ivory head of oriental origin (6th century B.C.) in case 21.

The exhibits in case 22 come from the sanctuary of Apollo, to whom warriors used to dedicate their spears or arrows. Among them are three iron spearheads and one of bronze, the latter made specially as an offering to the god, as the inscription informs us. There is also an interesting lead tablet with inscriptions on both sides recording the yearly income of the sanctuary. Case 20 contains a Corinthian figurine of the 6th century B.C., which was part of the decoration of a tripod: it represents a lion standing on a pedestal similar to an ionic capital. Other small bronzes of interest include a dove, a scorpion and some flowers. More or less in the centre of the room right behind the pediment above is one of the finest pieces in the museum, an Archaic lion which was found near the tomb of Menekrates but evidently does not belong to it, because it was made to fit a rectangular tomb. This majestic statue is by an unidentified Corinthian sculptor, obviously a very talented one, who worked at Korkyra at the end of the 7th century. Outstanding among the terracotta busts in case 13, which is near the lion, is a mask which probably represents Hermaphroditos (mid-5th century B.C.). The case next to it contains objects of later date, notably a fragment of a Megarian *skyphos* (two-handled drinking-cup) with a relief representation of a couple embracing (2nd century B.C.).

Case 19, against the opposite wall, contains some of the terracotta statuettes of Artemis which were found in large numbers during the excavation of the small sanctuary of Artemis, at Kanoni. Most of them represent the goddess holding her bow and a stag (c. 480 B.C.). The workmanship of these votive offerings is mediocre. Next there are some fragments from the terracotta decoration of the roof of a small 6th-century temple, also in the grounds of Mon Repos. Fragments of the terracotta statuettes from the pediment of the same building, which must have been an extremely attractive one, may be seen in case 18.

The pieces at the far end of this room are of various dates from the 4th century B.C. to the Roman period; most of them are sculptures standing on pedestals. Of the exhibits in show-cases, the most interesting are a small marble head of a Satyr, a beautifully-made mould of the head of a Negro (late Hellenistic period) with a cast placed next to it, and some Roman oil-lamps with representations in relief. Of the sculptures, note first the small but excellent copy (2nd century A.D.) of Apollo of the Kassel type; the original was the Apollo Parnopios by Phidias, a bronze statue which used to stand on the Acropolis in Athens. The marble head of a morose-looking man may be a copy of a portrait head of Thucydides, of 300 B.C.; this copy was made during the Roman period. The marble head of the comic poet Menander is a much better piece, being a copy of very fine workmanship dating from the 1st century B.C.; the original, a bronze by the sons of Praxiteles, was in the Theatre of Dionysos in Athens. Another portrait head, most probably of the philosopher Pyrrhon of Elis, is a copy (200 B.C.) of a bronze attributed to Lysippos (late 4th century B.C.). Then there is a small statue of a clothed Aphrodite resting her left elbow on statuette of a woman who is lifting her dress and showing her naked body (2nd century B.C.); and lastly a torso of Eros by the school of Praxiteles (4th century B.C.). A huge capital from the Temple of Artemis and a fragment of a column may be seen in the courtyard of the museum.

THE SINO-JAPANESE MUSEUM

This museum, the only one of its kind in Greece, is very well worth a visit. Some of the exhibits are of great importance and can be compared with the best oriental collections in museums abroad.

The museum is housed on the upper floor of the Palace of St Michael and St George, the architecture of which is described in the section on 19th-century buildings. The Palace itself is worth seeing for its own sake as a good example of Regency taste. The imposing great hall on the ground floor is adorned with two rows of Ionic columns with paintings of scenes from the Odyssey. At the far end is a broad, majestic stairway, branching into two flights about half-way up, which leads to the first-floor landing with its Corinthian colonnade. Facing the stairheads are the three staterooms of the Palace: the circular ballroom in the centre, the throne-room on the left and the banqueting-room on the right.

Most of the exhibits in the museum come to be there through the generosity of the Corfiot diplomat Grigorios Manos, who donated his 10,000-piece collection to the Greek State about thirty years ago. Another collection of about 200 pieces was donated by N. Hadjivassiliou, a former Greek ambassador in New Delhi, and two more, smaller still, by I. Siniossoglou and P. Almanakhou, both of whom were also in the diplomatic service.

Until recently some of the rooms in the museum were closed, but they are now all open to the public. Between them they provide a comprehensive picture of oriental art, covering all periods and all the regions of the Far East. The exhibits have been intelligently and tastefully laid out, in such a way as to show them to their best advantage without spoiling the character of the building. Some of the most interesting and important exhibits are mentioned below.

Starting in the room just to the left of the throne-room, in the east wing, we find bronzes of the Shang dynasty (1500—1027 B.C.), the dawn of the historical era in China; earthenware vases of the Chou dynasty (1027—221 B.C.); a good collection from the Han dynasty (221 B.C.—A.D. 220) — the period of Chinese political unification, when the arts flourished — including a charming model of a house, which gives a good illustration of contemporary architecture, and a number of statues; some fine terracotta tomb statuettes of the T'ang dynasty (618—907), of exquisite delicacy; and a seated bronze Buddha of the Sung dynasty (960—1279).

The second room contains examples of the art of the Ming dynasty

(1368—1644), which was the golden age of all the arts in China and the great heyday of Confucianism: bronze vases; statuettes of sandstone or porcelain; ivory miniatures (in a small showcase of their own); statuettes, small vases and other articles made of bronze with exquisite cloisonné enamel decoration; and very fine porcelain vases in the characteristic Chinese blue. From this room there is a splendid view of the Venetian wall and the sea.

Room Γ contains various pieces dating from the Ch'ing dynasty (1644—1912), including 18th-century miniatures made of semi-precious stones (rock crystal, amethyst, amber and jade). Out-standing among them are the magnificent ivory figurines and the mother-of-pearl relief in the third showcase from the left.

Most of the contents of Room Δ are porcelains of the same (Ch'ing) dynasty. Note especially the curious porcelain painted to suit European tastes, with such unlikely subjects as coats of arms and nude women. In the middle of the room are four low cases containing charming phials made of porcelain and semiprecious stones.

Room E is the only one with Chinese furniture, which dates from the same period as the contents of the two preceding rooms. It also contains textiles and costumes, as well as a portrait (on paper) of the last empress of the Ch'ing dynasty.

In Room Z we move on to Japanese art. The oldest of the exhibits belong to the earliest period of Japanese history, the Ya-yoi period (250 B.C.—A.D. 250). Note the statuettes of the Kamakura period (1192—1338), and particularly the wood-carving of a fierce temple custodian. Room H, which leads back on to the landing, contains another collection of Japanese pieces, including weapons and samurai armour (16th-18th cent.), actors' masks used in the Nō theatre, which flourished in the Muramashi or Asikaga period (1338—1578), and, over the mantelpiece, a picture from the Kabuki popular theatre. (It is worth mentioning, incidentally, that the fireplaces are different in every room of the Palace: some of them are very fine.). Between two showcases containing bronze vases and statuettes stands a lovely screen with a picture of Samurai warriors on horseback.

From the central landing go into Room Θ, the floridly-decorated throne-room, which was used by the Lords High Commissioners for official audiences. This contains, among other things, two huge paintings of St Michael and St Gabriel and a portrait of King George I of Greece.

A doorway out of Room Θ, takes you into Room I, the round, domed ballroom, which has four niches each containing a statue of a Muse. All four of them are plaster casts from the same mould, which means that one is confronted by four images of the same lady — a distinctly mediocre piece of sculpture — with no difference between them except for a slight variation in the angle of view! Some low showcases in this room contain specimens of Japanese miniature work such as *inro* (small medicine-caskets), which were fastened on to the kimono sache with ornamental toggles called *netsuke* (17th-19th cent.).

Room K, which comes next, is a vast room — the biggest in the museum — which used to be the banqueting room and is decorated in the colours of the Order of St Michael and St George. It contains a variety of exhibits from Japan, dating from the 17th-19th centuries: ceramics, lacquered wooden articles, inkwells and other writing materials, fans, prints (18th-19th cent.) showing scenes of everyday life, and much else of interest.

Room Π, on the right of the stairs from the ground floor contains a variety of Indian wood-carvings including some erotic ones with religious symbolism (18th-19th cent.). Outstanding among the painted Korean screens are one with a picture of a scholar's library (16th cent.) and one by the left wall with a very beautiful painting of the Chinese palace (14th cent.). Then there are two Khmer heads from Cambodia, on individual pedestals, and a showcase of Thai sculpture.

Next comes Room O, which has a most interesting collection of pieces illustrating the development of Indian art from the early centuries of the Christian era up to the 19th century.

Off the landing to the right of Room Π is Room Λ, where it is worth looking at the Japanese screens and the very interesting sculptures from Gandhara in N.W. India (renowned for its Hellenic Buddhist school), with their markedly Hellenistic elements, and from Nepal and Tibet. Outstanding among the Tibetan pieces are the bronze statuettes of the numerous gods of the Lamaistic pantheon.

COLLECTION OF CHRISTIAN ART

From there we move on to the **Collection of Christian Art,** still in the same wing of the Palace. The first room contains Early Christian architectural sculptures and fragments of mosaic floors from the church at Paleopolis. Next come some fragments of Byzantine wall-paintings stripped from the walls of the ruined church of Aghios Nikolaos at Kato Korakiana (11th, 13th and 18th cent.). Lastly there is a collection of icons of the 16th and 18th centuries, comprising major works of this period which have been brought here from various town churches. It is only possible to mention a few representative examples: SS Sergius and Bacchus by M. Damaskinos; St John the Baptist by E. Lombardos; St Nicholas with scenes from his life by Th. Poulakis; St John of Damascus by Ioannis Tzenos; St Cyril, Patriarch of Alexandria (from the Church of SS Jason and Sosipater) by E. Tzane Bounialis; the archangels Gabriel, Michael and Raphael by Georgios Kortezas. St John the Hermit with scenes from his life is a work by Ieremias Palladas, painted in the 17th century but still close to the old tradition. An icon of St Demetrios on a red horse presents an interesting combination of the two trends which dominated the art of this period: the saint is painted in the Byzantine style but the details of his horse are derived from Italian art.

OTHER COLLECTIONS

In Odos Akadimias, which leads off to the west from the south end of the Spianada by the imposing shell of the ruined Ionian Academy (originally a Venetian barrack-block, as already mentioned), is the newly-opened **Municipal Art Gallery.** It occupies the ground floor of a fine old building (Dalietos Bequest) which has been tastefully renovated. Old maps of Corfu are hung in the entrance hall and some of the corridors. The first room on the right is devoted to portraits of Greek royalty. In the next room there are two very fine post-Byzantine icons from the church of the First Cemetery (which, as we have seen, still has several other icons of excellent quality) and a painting of the assassination of President Ioannis Kapodistrias at Nafplion, a subject well-known from other paintings. Then come several rooms with works by some of the best-known Corfiot painters. Lastly there is the Baxter Collection, an extremely interesting set of pictures by an English lady artist and botanist of that name who made a comprehensive, meticulous and beautifully illustrated study of the flora of Corfu. The most attractive works in this collection are her pictures of the wild flowers that grow on the island's hillsides and in its fields, such as the many different species and varieties of crocus.

An excellent collection of paintings belonging to the **Corfu Literary Society** is unfortunately not yet open to the public: a pity, but at least it provides yet another incentive for planning a return visit to the island!

THE ARCHAEOLOGICAL MUSEUM

90. One of the leopanthers (fabulous beasts with the head of a lion and the body of a panther) which flank the main group of figures in the Gorgon pediment.

91. The Gorgon, the central figure of the pediment is shown running towards the right with her kness bent in the conventional style of Archaic art. Even carved in stone, her monstrous features are a spine-chilling sight.

94

92. The Gorgon
pediment from the
doric temple of
Artemis (590-580
B.C.) is the work of a
Corinthian artist; it
is the oldest stone
pediment on a large
scale found in
Greece.

93, 94. The two
felines, known as
"leopanthers", flank
the central theme of
the Gorgon and
symbolize the powers
of nature.

95. The battle of
Gods and Titans,
from the right half of
the Gorgon pediment.
Zeus, shown here as
a beardless youth, is
hurling a thunderbolt
at a Titan.

96. Chrysaor, one of
the Gorgon's two
sons, is considered to
be one of the finest of
all Archaic
sculptures.

97. Detail from the large pediment of the temple of Artemis. The two terrible snakes girdle the waist of Gorgon.

98. The Archaic lion found near the Tomb of Menekrates. It is by a Corinthian sculptor who was working at Kerkyra in the late 7th century. Stylized though it is, it nevertheless gives the impression of being just about to spring on its prey.

99. *Head of a small Kouros, a corinthian work found in the area of Mon Repos (circa 530 B.C.).*

100. *Roman copy of a head, probably of the historian Thucydides, after an original dating from 300 B.C.*

101. *Head of Menander, the Athenian comic playwright. Copy of an important bronze by Cephisodotos and Timarchos, the sons of Praxiteles.*

99

100

101

 102

103

102, 103. Bronze lions, part of the decoration of two 6th cent. B.C. tripods.

104. Bronze statuette of a running reveller, holding a rhyton in his left hand. A laconian work, part of the decoration of a large bronze cauldron (circa 570 B.C.).

104

105. *St John the Hermit and scenes from his life. 17th cent.*

106. *St Nicolas surrounded by ten scenes with themes from his life. By Th. Poulakis (17th cent.).*

106

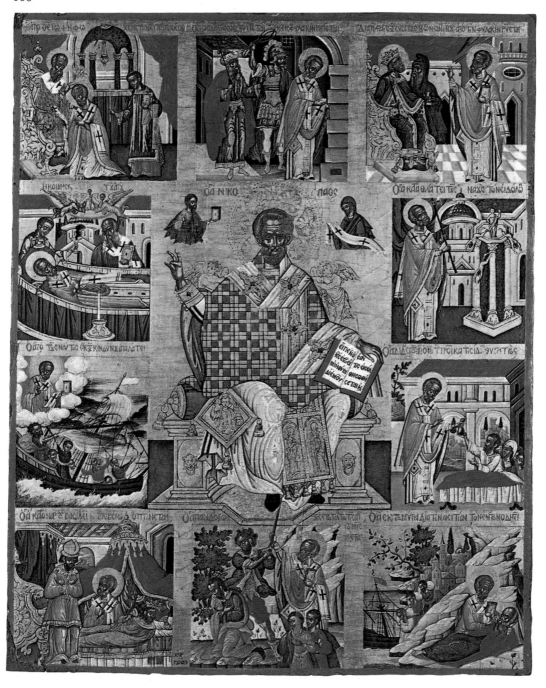

THE SINO-JAPANESE MUSEUM

107, 108. The T'ang period (618-907), which saw a considerable increase in China's political and economic power, was also a time of exceptional achievement in the arts. The charming ladies illustrated here accompanied a dead man into the grave. They exemplify just one of the many subjects depicted in tomb statuettes by the anonymous artists of this period. Manos Collection.

109. This bronze ritual cauldron of the Ming dynasty (1368-1644), which from an artistic point of view was one of the most brilliant periods in Chinese history, typifies the sublime level of attainment reached by Chinese metalworkers. Manos Collection.

107

108

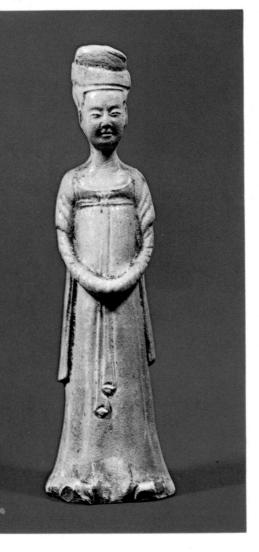

110

111

110, 111. Of the three religions or philosophical systems which have flourished in China, two — Confucianism and Taoism — were native products, while the third — Buddhism — was introduced from India. Religion played a very important part, both in the organization of government and in everyday life, in every period of Chinese history. Shown here are two statuettes of Chinese deities dating from the Ming dynasty (1368-1644). Manos Collection.

112. By the end of the 12th century the Samurai had consolidated their hold on Japan. The Kamakura period (1192-1338) saw considerable changes in all aspects of life and new trends in art with realism coming to the fore. The photograph shows a temple custodian made of wood. Manos Collection.

113, 114. Chinese art of the Ch'ing dynasty (1644-1912) was based on the tradition and introduced few new elements. Its predominant characteristic is technical perfection, even though there was a steep increase in output, particularly of porcelain and of miniatures made of ivory and semi-precious stones. Left: Jasper statuette of an official. Right: Gilded ivory statuette of a priest. Manos Collection.

115. Jasper statuette of an official. Ch'ing dynasty (1644-1912). Manos Collection.

113

114

116. Buddhism spread to the remotest parts of the Himalayas, where a new sect, Lamaism, was eventually developed from it. Many of the Buddhist deities were assimilated into the Lamaistic pantheon, including the wise and holy Bodhisattvas, who are portrayed in a wide variety of forms. Here we see a Bodhisattva made of bronze, gilded and inlaid with turquoise. Nepal, 14th cent. Manos Collection.

117. The gods and goddesses of Hinduism, the most widespread religion in India, have an infinite number of reincarnations, and each one has his or her own sacred beast symbolizing the animal attributes of the deity in question. The god Siva symbolizes the unending conflict to be found in nature: he is both the destroyer and the preserver of life and the world. His sacred animal is the bull Nandi. The Picture shows a bull of the Siva family, made of bronze and copper. Gangajummi group, 17th cent. Hadjivassiliou Collection.

118. Sculpture in the Himalayas most commonly takes the form of bronze statuettes. One goddess very frequently represented is the White Tara, shown here. Nepal, 17th cent. Hadjivassiliou Collection.

116

117

119

120

119. *Under the Ch'ing dynasty (1644-1912) porcelain output rose to an unprecedent level, partly as a result of the increased demand for Chinese porcelain in the West. Shown here is a porcelain phial. Manos Collection.*

120. *In the K'ang Hsi period (1662-1722) the Chinese made porcelain wares which were very popular in Europe, where they were classified into families according to the predominant colour of their decorative designs. Here we see a plate with* **famille verte** *decoration. Manos Collection.*

121. *The porcelain vase shown here belongs to the* **famille rose** *which is later than the* **famille verte** *illustrated in Fig. 120. Ch'ing dynasty (1644-1912). Siniossoglou Collection.*

121

122. One of the art forms in which the Japanese produced their most successful and expressive results was painted screens of varying sizes. This photograph shows part of a two-leaved screen with a painting of Samurai of the Edo period (1615-1867), which is so called because it was then that the seat of government was moved to Edo, the modern Tokyo. Manos Collection.

123. Part of a four-leaved screen with a painting of a sea-battle. Japan, Edo period (1615-1867). Hadjivassiliou Collection.

123

157

124. Part of a two-leaved screen decorated with paintings of flowers of the four seasons. Japan, Edo period (1615-1867). Hadjivassiliou Collection.

125. Occupying a prominent position in the art of the Himalayas are the **thangkas,** sacred painted banners which usually depict scenes from the lives of the Lamaistic deities. The **thangka** shown here dates from the 17th or 18th century. Hadjivassiliou Collection.

BIBLIOGRAPHY

ΑΓΟΡΟΠΟΥΛΟΥ-ΜΠΙΡΜΠΙΛΗ, Α., Ἡ Ἀρχιτεκτονική τῆς πόλεως τῆς Κερκύρας κατά τήν περίοδο τῆς Ἐνετοκρατίας. Athens 1977.

ΑΣΠΙΩΤΗ, Μ., Τό ἀνάκτορο τῶν Ἁγίων Μιχαήλ καί Γεωργίου. Corfu 1964.

ΒΟΚΟΤΟΠΟΥΛΟΣ, Π. Λ., Περί τήν χρονολόγησιν τοῦ ἐν Κερκύρα ναοῦ τῶν Ἁγ. Ἰάσονος καί Σωσιπάτρου. Δελτίον Χριστιανικῆς Ἀρχαιολογικῆς Ἐταιρίας 5 (1969), 149-172.
— Ἡ βυζαντινή τέχνη στά Ἑπτάνησα. Κερκυραϊκά Χρονικά XV (1970), 148-180.
— Fresques datées du XIᵉ siècle à Corfou. Cahiers Archéologiques 21 (1970), 151-180.
— Βυζαντινά καί μεσαιωνικά μνημεῖα Ἰονίων νήσων. Ἀρχαιολογικόν Δελτίον 22 (1967), B 371-376, 23 (1968), B 302-324, 25 (1970), B 333-346.

ΔΑΦΝΗΣ, Κ., Τά κάστρα τῆς Κέρκυρας. Κερκυραϊκά Χρονικά I (1951), 17-24.

DINSMOOR, W.B., The Kardaki temple re-examined. Athenische Mitteilungen 88 (1973), 165-174.

ΔΟΝΤΑΣ, Γ., A Guide to the archaelogical Museum of Corfou. Athens 1972.
— Ἀρχαιότητες καί μνημεῖα Ἰονίων νήσων. Ἀρχαιολογικόν Δελτίον 18 (1963), B 161-186, 20 (1965), B2 378-400, 21 (1966), B2 316-330 (καί Π. ΚΑΛΛΙΓΑΣ) 22 (1967), B2 360-370.
— Ἀνασκαφαί Κερκύρας. Πρακτικά (1965), 66-77, (1966), 85-94.
— Τοπογραφικά θέματα τῆς πολιορκίας τῆς Κερκύρας τοῦ ἔτους 373 π.Χ. Ἀρχαιολογική Ἐφημερίς (1965), 139-144.
— Le Grand Sanctuaire de Mon Repos à Corfu. Ἀρχαιολογικά Ἀνάλεκτα ἐξ Ἀθηνῶν (1968), 66-69.
— Die griechischen Inseln, 396-402. Evi Melas (ed) 1976.

ΙΣΤΟΡΙΑ ΤΟΥ ΕΛΛΗΝΙΚΟΥ ΕΘΝΟΥΣ. Ἐκδοτική Ἀθηνῶν. Α—ΣΤ, I—ΙΔ 1970-1979.

JOHNSON F.B. - W.B. DINSMOOR, The Kardaki temple. American Journal of Archaeology 40 (1936), 46.

ΚΑΛΛΙΓΑΣ, Π., The archaeological site of Paleopolis in Kerkyra. Ἀρχαιολογικά Ἀνάλεκτα ἐξ Ἀθηνῶν III (1970), 285-287.
— Τό ἐν Κερκύρα ἱερόν τῆς Ἀκραίας Ἥρας. Ἀρχαιολογικόν Δελτίον 24 (1969), A 51-58, 24 (1969), B 258-268.
— An inscribed lead plaque from Kerkyra. Annual of the British school of Athens 66 (1971), 79-94.
— Κερκυραία Μάστιξ. Ἀρχαιολογικά Ἀνάλεκτα ἐξ Ἀθηνῶν IX (1976), 61-67.
— Μνημεῖα τῆς νεώτερης Κέρκυρας. Ἀρχαιολογικόν Δελτίον 21 (1966), A 158-162.

ΚΑΛΛΙΠΟΛΙΤΗΣ, Β., Ἱστορικοί σταθμοί τῆς Κερκυραϊκῆς Παλαιόπολης. Corfu 1958.
— Ἀνασκαφή ἐν Παλαιοπόλει τῆς Κερκύρας. Πρακτικά (1955), 187-192, (1956), 158-163, (1957), 79-84, (1959), 115-119, (1961), 120-128.

ΚΑΤΣΑΡΟΣ, Σ., Χρονικά τῶν Κορυφῶν. Corfu 1976.

ΚΟΛΛΑΣ, Ι.Δ., Ἡ ἀρχιτεκτονική σφραγίδα τῆς προστασίας. Κερκυραϊκά Χρονικά I (1951), 30-34.

ΚΩΣΤΟΓΛΟΥ — ΔΕΣΠΙΝΗ, Κ., Ἀνασκαφή εἰς Κασσιόπη Κερκύρας. Ἀρχαιολογικά Ἀνάλεκτα ἐξ Ἀθηνῶν (1971), 202-206 (καί Π. ΑΓΑΛΛΟΠΟΥΛΟΥ), Ἀρχαιότητες καί μνημεῖα Ἰονίων νήσων. Ἀρχαιολογικόν Δελτίον 26 (1971), B 344-358.

ΛΙΝΑΡΔΟΥ, Γ., Τό Ἀγγελόκαστρο Κερκύρας. Κερκυραϊκά Χρονικά XX (1976), 9-53.

ΛΟΥΝΤΖΗΣ, Ε., Περί τῆς πολιτικῆς καταστάσεως τῆς Ἑπτανήσου ἐπί Ἐνετῶν. (Athens 1969).

MARMORAS, A., Della historia di Corfou. Venezia 1972, Corfou 1902.

MATTON, R., Corfou. Athens 1960.

MILLER, W., The Latines in the Levant. (Cambridge — N. York 1964²).

ΞΥΓΓΟΠΟΥΛΟΥ Α. - Ι. ΠΑΠΑΔΗΜΗΤΡΙΟΥ, Ἔρευναι ἐν Παλαιοπόλει τῆς Κερκύρας. Πρακτικά (1936), 99-110.

ΠΑΠΑΔΗΜΗΤΡΙΟΥ, Ι., Ὁ ναός τῶν Ἁγίων Ἰάσονος καί Σωσιπάτρου ἐν Κερκύρα. Ἀρχαιολογική Ἐφημερίς (1934-35), 37-56.
— Ὁ Ἰοβιανός τῆς βασιλικῆς τῆς Παλαιοπόλεως. Ἀρχαιολογική Ἐφημερίς (1942-4), (Χρονικά) 39-48. Ἀνασκαφή ἐν Κερκύρα. Πρακτικά (1939), 92-99.

RANGAVIS, E.P., Livre d'or de la noblesse Ionienne. Corfu 1925.

RHOMAIOS, K., Les premières fouilles de Corfou. Bulletin de Correspondence Hellenique (1925), 190-218.

RODENWALDT, G., Altdorische Bilwerke in Korfou. Berlin 1938.
— Kerkyra. Archaishe Bauten und Bildwerke. II Die Bildwerke des Artemistempels. Berlin 1939.

SCHLEIF, H.-K. RHOMAIOS - G. KLAFFENBACH, Korkyra. Archaische Bauten und Bilwerke. I Der Artemis tempel. Berlin 1940.

SORDINAS, A., Investigations of the Prehistory of Corfu during 1964-66. Balkan studies 10 (1969), 393-424.

STAMATOPOULOS, N., Old Corfu. A brief Artistic and Historical Survey. Corfu 1978².

ΤΣΙΤΣΑΣ, Λ., Ἡ ἐκκλησία τῆς Κερκύρας κατά τήν Λατινοκρατία. Corfu 1969.

YOUNG, M., Corfu and the other Ionian islands. London 1973.

ΧΑΤΖΗΔΑΚΗΣ, Μ., Ἀρχιτεκτονική Ἑπτανήσου. Ἱστορία τοῦ Ἑλληνικοῦ Ἔθνους. Ἐκδοτική Ἀθηνῶν I, 415

ΧΩΡΕΜΗΣ, Α., Ἀρχαϊκόν ἀέτωμα ἐκ Κερκύρας. Ἀρχαιολογικά Ἀνάλεκτα ἐξ Ἀθηνῶν VII (1974), 183-186.

ACKNOWLEDGEMENTS

The publishers wish to thank his Excellency the British Ambassador in Creece for permission to photograph paintings in the British Embassy in Athens. Also the Ephor of Antiquities for Corfu Mr. A. Choremis, the Epimelete of Byzantine Antiquities Mr. D. Triantaphyllopoulos and the Epimelete Mrs. A. Karamanou-Papoutsani for their help during the preparation of this quidebook. Thanks are also due to Dr. A. Agoropoulou-Birbili for granting permission to reprint certain drawings from her book. The maps were prerared by Tonia Kotsoni.